# The Homebrewed Christianity Guide to Church History

# The Homebrewed Christianity Guide to Church History

## Flaming Heretics and Heavy Drinkers

BILL LEONARD
AUTHOR

TRIPP FULLER
SERIES EDITOR

Fortress Press
Minneapolis

THE HOMEBREWED CHRISTIANITY GUIDE TO CHURCH HISTORY
Flaming Heretics and Heavy Drinkers



Cover design: Jesse Turri
Book design: PerfecType, Nashville, TN

Print ISBN: 978-1-5064-0574-2
eBook ISBN: 978-1-5064-0575-9

The paper used in this publication meets the minimum requirements of American National Standard for Information Sciences — Permanence of Paper for Printed Library Materials, ANSI Z329.48-1984.

Manufactured in the U.S.A.

To the students and graduates of the School of Divinity,
Wake Forest University, 1999–2018, ever a "shelter
for those distressed of conscience." Homebrewed
Christianity extraordinaire.

# Contents

# Series Introduction

You are about to read a guidebook. Not only is the book the sweet "guide book" size, shaped perfectly to take a ride in your back pocket, but the book itself was crafted with care by a real-deal theology nerd. Here's the thing. The Homebrewed Christianity Guide series has one real goal: we want to think *with* you, not *for* you.

The whole "homebrew" metaphor grows from my passion for helping anyone who wants to geek out about theology to do so with the best ingredients around. That's why I started the Homebrewed Christianity podcast in 2008, and that's why I am thrilled to partner with Fortress Press's Theology for the People team to produce this series. I am confident that the church has plenty of intelligent and passionate people who want a more robust conversation about their faith.

A podcast, in case you're wondering, is like talk radio on demand without the commercials. You download a file and listen when, if, where, and how long you want. I love the podcast medium. Short of talking one-on-one, there's hardly a more intimate presence than speaking to someone in their earbuds as they're stuck in traffic, on the treadmill, or washing dishes. When I started the podcast,

I wanted to give anyone the option of listening to some of the best thinkers from the church and the academy.

Originally, the podcast was for friends, family, and my local pub theology group. I figured people in the group were more likely to listen to a podcast than read a giant book. So as the resident theology nerd, I read the books and then interviewed the authors. Soon, thousands of people were listening. Since then the audience has grown to over fifty thousand unique listeners each month and over a million downloads. A community of listeners, whom we call Deacons, grew, and we've got a cast of co-hosts and regular guests.

Over the better part of a decade, I have talked to scores of theologians and engaged with the Deacons about these conversations. It has been a real joy. Every time I hear from a listener, I do the happy dance in my soul.

And here's the deal: I love theology, but I love the church more. I am convinced that the church can really make a difference in the world. But in order to do that, it needs to face reality rather than run from it. The church must use its brain, live its faith, and join God in working for the salvation of the world. And that's what these books are all about.

We often open and close the podcast by reminding listeners that we are providing the ingredients so that they can brew their own faith. That's the same with these books. Each author is an expert theological brewer, and they've been asked to write from their own point of view. These guidebooks are not boringly neutral; instead, they are zestily provocative, meant to get you thinking and brewing.

I look forward to hearing from you on the Speakpipe at HomebrewedChristianity.com and meeting you at an HBC 3D event. We can drink a pint and talk about this book, how you agree and disagree with it. Because if we're talking about theology, the world is a better place.

And remember: Share the Brew!

Tripp Fuller

# The Homebrewed Posse

Whether it's the podcast, the blog, or live events, Homebrewed Christianity has always been a conversation, and these books are no different. So inside of this and every volume in the HBC book, you'll be hearing from four members of the Homebrewed community. They are:

**The Bishop:** Kindly, pastoral, encouraging. She's been around the block a few times, and nothing ruffles her feathers. She wants everyone to succeed, and she's an optimist, so she knows they will.

**The Elder:** Scolding, arrogant, know-it-all. He's old and disgruntled, the father figure you can never please. He loves quoting doctrine; he's the kind of guy who controls every church meeting because he knows Roberts Rules of Order better than anyone else.

THE DEACON

**The Deacon:** Earnest, excited, energetic. He's a guy who has just discovered HBC, and he can't get enough of it. He's a cheerleader, a shouter, an encourager. He's still in his first naïveté.

THE ACOLYTE

**The Acolyte:** Smart, inquisitive, skeptical. She's the smartest student in your confirmation class. She's bound to be a biologist or a physicist, and she's skeptical of all the hocus pocus of Christianity. But she hasn't given up on it yet, so her questions come from the heart. She really wants to know if all this stuff works.

We look forward to continuing the conversation with you, online and in-person!

# 1

# Herding Ecclesiastical Cats

*"Thou art Peter, and upon this rock I will build my church, and the gates of hell shall not prevail against it."*

Jesus Christ to Simon Peter

*"He can no longer have God for his Father, who has not the Church for his Mother."*

Cyprian of Carthage

*"God wills that we take ourselves with great strength to the faith of holy Church and find there our most precious mother in comfort and true understanding with the whole communion of blessed ones."*

Julian of Norwich

*"Farewell to those who want an entirely pure and purified church. This is plainly wanting no church at all."*

Martin Luther

*"Better to be cast out of the church than to deny Christ."*

Ann Hutchinson

*"Going to church doesn't make you a Christian any more than going to a garage makes you an automobile."*

Billy Sunday

*"If the church does not recapture its prophetic zeal, it will become an irrelevant social club without spiritual or moral authority."*

Martin Luther King Jr.

*"The church is like Noah's ark. It stinks, but if you get out of it, you'll drown."*

Shane Claiborne

*"Describe church history. Use both sides of the paper if necessary."*

Charlie Brown

## Hep him, Jesus, hep him!

It was my first serpent handling, up a hollow from Berea, Kentucky, on a blazing hot Sunday in June 1990. Our group of faculty and students from a summer Appalachian studies program joined Reverend Arnold Saylor and his family for an outdoor family reunion, revival service, serpent handling, and dinner-on-the-ground. The three-hour worship service included Holy Ghost singing and preaching, punctuated by the handling of serpents based on a particular reading of texts from the Gospel of Mark, chapter sixteen. (The snakes were mostly timber rattlers, kept in a padlocked box with a cross emblazoned across the top.)

The first preacher, a young man apparently just beginning to cultivate his pulpit skills, "took the stand" and held forth. His discourse was barely underway before we all knew it was not going well. The Pentecostal power seemed to elude him at every rhetorical turn. His outdoor congregants attempted a homiletical rescue operation, urging him on, feeding him assorted Bible verses and hallelujahs, rejoicing when the Spirit broke through, even momentarily. Finally, when it became clear to just about everyone that he really couldn't preach a lick, as they say, a woman in the crowd called out: "Hep him, Jesus, hep him." Well, even Jesus couldn't hep him that day, so again the women intervened, one of them picking up a guitar and starting to sing. It was, I learned later, an old-time Appalachian revival-ritual called "singing them down," a congregational way of letting preachers know that they'd run their course, rescuing them from continued sermonic catastrophe. A second, more seasoned preacher took over, demonstrating considerably more style and content than his younger colleague, even handling a serpent during part of his sermon, an act like nothing I'd ever seen before, with a group of people who welcomed our group of outsiders with kindness.

The next fall I related that story to my Christian History class at the Southern Baptist Theological Seminary, Louisville, where I was then teaching. Later in the semester, in a discussion of medieval scholasticism and the thought of St. Thomas Aquinas, the "Angelic Doctor" of Catholic theology, I fumbled an explanation of his ontological argument for the existence of God. Finally, in collective desperation, a student in the back of the room called out, "Well, hep him, Jesus, hep him!" Class dismissed.

---

THE ELDER

There is a clear dividing line among churches—those that handle snakes and those that appreciate the ontological argument.

---

## Homebrewed History

"Hep him, Jesus," is a good phrase, maybe even a good prayer, to invoke at the beginning of this study. The editors of the *Homebrewed Christianity* series, my friends Tripp Fuller and Tony Jones, were only slightly more expansive in their directives than that of the latter-day philosopher/theologian Charlie Brown, whose comment helps introduce the book. Tripp and Tony counseled: "Describe church history. Use 40,000 words; 50,000 if necessary!" Yes, "hep him Jesus" is a worthy place to embark on such a daunting task.

Their invitation to *guide* readers through two thousand years of Christian history offered a provocative challenge, whatever the word limit. On one hand, historical purists may fret that such a brief volume inevitably requires omission of otherwise essential information; as in, "How can you discuss Logos Christology and omit Patripassianism?" (We'll explore both movements, but all too briefly.) On the other hand, even the briefest *guide* may seem information overload for those who admit that they've "never really gotten into the history thing," or for whom historical studies are a kind of late-night, academic Ambien. (As a student in my British Religious Dissent course blurted out on exiting Westminster Abbey, "Prof, I'm maxed out on cathedrals!")

Sorting through all those names and dates, ideas and doctrines, creeds and conversions, heretics and inquisitors (be they drunk or sober), can become immediately mind-numbing for students needing just three more credits for graduation ("Will this be on the test?"); for history buffs, obsessed with ecclesiastical minutia ("Did Martin Luther really throw an ink bottle at the Devil?"); or for postmodern seekers titillated by the subtitle *flaming heretics*, *heavy drinkers*, and the potential for keeping Christianity weird ("Did Teresa of Avila really envision a beautiful angel carrying a spear?"). There is a lot to tell.

## What This Book Is (and Is Not)

Let's be clear. This book is not a history of the Christian church. Rather, it is a *guide* for reflecting on *how* we might study history individually and collectively. A *guide* offers certain clues for organizing, analyzing, and yes, even challenging, various beliefs, practices, and controversies that formed and still inform Christian individuals and communities. From my way of thinking, such a *guide* is worth doing because the church's legacy is so endlessly beguiling—enduring accounts of a host of saintly and idiosyncratic individuals (often the same persons) who wrestled with assorted beliefs and practices for explaining, experiencing, and contradicting the life and teaching, death and continuing presence of Jesus of Nazareth, who became to the church, the Son of the living God. This *guide* offers various ways of approaching a vast array of persons, movements, dogmas, debates that developed in response to Jesus, who he was, is, and will be, world without end. Amen.

## Flaming Heretics and Heavy Drinkers: Christianity on the Margins

Hence the strange, wondrous (and assigned) subtitle—*flaming heretics and heavy drinkers*, carrying us to the margins and the marginalized of the Christian story. Flaming heretics abound in Christian history. Ideas deemed on or over the edge of orthodoxy led to the denunciation, excommunication, imprisonment, or execution of multitudes. Burning, drowning, and beheading were the three methods of choice for medieval heretics, with burning at the stake the most heinously cruel, particularly when they used green wood. Heresy had to be punished, so the story goes, to preserve the cultural and doctrinal veracity of the "one true Church."

Yet in the irony of it all—and church history is full of irony—today's heretic is often (but not always) tomorrow's saint. Indeed, the church is full of sacred embarrassments, persons reviled in their day as destructive to truth, justice, and the ecclesiastical or political status quo. This great cloud of witnesses includes dissenters the likes of Polycarp and Perpetua, Montanus, Arius, Peter Waldo, John Hus, Balthasar Hubmaier, Felix Mantz, Thomas Müntzer, Sor Juana de la Cruz, Roger Williams, Ann Hutchinson, Ann Lee, Oscar Romero, Dietrich Bonhoeffer, and Martin Luther King Jr., to list only a few. These individuals, reviled in their day, sometimes paying with their lives, became icons of the faith for future generations. So this

---

I tell confirmands that a saint is someone the church points back to as having been faithful. Saints don't feel like saints. They become saints in our remembering.

**THE BISHOP**

---

particular *guide to church history* suggests that in the ecclesiastical scheme of things, the *flaming heretics* have frequently offered some of most insightful and/or bizarre ways of being and believing in the Christian church.

And that's not all. The details of the dead past, the dogmas borne of "corpse-cold orthodoxy," are not merely arcane trinkets to be collected or systematized by and for the theological dilettante. They are worth taking seriously, not only for the times in which they occurred, but as potential *guides* for who we have been and don't want to be again; or reminders of what we've lost and need to recover (or run away from like the plague). While the soaring triumphs and roaring failures are worth examining in their own historical contexts, we might find them helpful in our own struggles to "read" the church's present and future. For example, has the twenty-first-century church finally moved beyond the seventeenth-century doggerel: "When women preach and peasants pray, the fiends in hell make holiday," or does it perpetuate subtler forms of that misogynistic, hierarchal mantra?

---

THE ELDER

I am pretty sure there is a silent policy in most churches that we will support women's ordination, just as long as they go preach at another church.

---

Likewise, any decent *guide* to church history forces us to acknowledge that present events and contemporary contexts inform and profoundly shape the way we read and interpret the past. Amid current condemnation of the actions of Islamic radicals for burning, hanging, and beheading their "infidel" enemies in the name of God, we Christians are compelled to revisit our own history of burnings, hangings, and beheadings in the name of Father, Son, and Holy Ghost. We read the past, even as we struggle with ways in which the past reads us.

And what of *heavy drinkers*? Perhaps that phrase captures the earthiness that is inherent in even the life of the holiest individuals. St. Paul advised: "Be not drunk with wine, wherein is excess, but be filled with the Spirit." Yet he or someone like him advised the younger Timothy to "Take a little wine for your stomach's sake." To provide a *guide* to reading, perhaps even understanding the church's history is to acknowledge that there are always rules, and that those rules are often modified at best, ignored at worst. The history of the church is a study in human beings, some of whom keep the rules and others who get a little (or a lot) out of hand. Whether in a predetermined spiritual condition (original sin/total depravity), or as a sign of unbridled free will, human frailty, sinfulness, and yes, human evil, can find its way into every heart and every institution all too readily.

---

Denying the worst of our history, be it an institution like the church, a nation, or even our own life, is setting us up for failure.

**THE DEACON**

---

To speak of *heavy drinkers* in Christian history is to recall a group of knightly cronies, drinking their way toward morning with England's King Henry II, who think they hear their liege-lord-pal ask: "Who will rid me of this meddlesome monk?" Assuming that alcohol-laced comment as a drunken mandate to assassinate Henry's best-friend-turned-nemesis Thomas Becket, the Archbishop of Canterbury, the knights committed murder in the cathedral, December 29, 1170, creating one of the great martyr-saints of the Middle Ages.

Today I think we just have heavy-drinking bloggers regretting their late-night tweeting.

Then, as now, obsessions with body and spirit, whether alcohol- or fanaticism-induced, can lead to all kinds of ecclesiastical excesses, from burning, drowning, or beheading heretics and social nonconformists, to armed crusades against theological and cultural enemies (Cathari, Muslims, Waldensians), to the use of Holy Scripture to support chattel slavery. When it comes to the history of the Christian church, the phrase *heavy drinkers* represents more than simply too many bottles of brandy-wine. Being "drunk with the Spirit" can produce inspired prophets or dangerous fanatics. It's a very thin line.

## The Folks on the Margins: "They" and "We"—Then and Now

Again, let's not forget the dangerous people on the margins. Consider this third-century warning to the "true" church:

> They have been deceived by two females, Priscilla and Maximilla by name, whom they hold to be prophetesses, asserting that into them the Paraclete spirit entered. . . . They magnify these females above the Apostles and every gift of Grace, so that some of them go so far as to say that

> there is in them something more than Christ. . . . These people agree with the Church in acknowledging the Father of the universe to be God and Creator of all things, and they also acknowledge all that the Gospel testifies of Christ. But they introduce novelties in the form of fasts and feasts, abstinences and diets of radishes, giving these females as their authority.[1]

Thus Hippolytus, bishop of Rome, described the beginnings of the Montanist movement in Asia Minor (Phrygia) and its claims that the Holy Spirit could anoint female prophets as readily as males, inspiring them to create "novelties" inappropriate to "the [normative] Church." Hippolytus conceded the group's orthodoxy regarding the nature of the Godhead, at least where Father-Creator and Christ were concerned. But he insisted they clearly were deceived about the Paraclete; led astray by the two false "prophetesses" whose heretical revelations might well have been shaped by their continued gorging on radishes! Eusebius, the fourth-century church historian, echoed Hippolytus's condemnation, accusing the Montanists of manifesting a "bastard spirit so that they uttered demented, absurd and irresponsible sayings."[2]

The Montanists illustrate this abiding reality: *Throughout the history of the Christian Church, normative belief and practice remains a moveable feast.* In every era, a variety of individuals and movements are sure to appear, occupying or exiled to the theological, liturgical, doctrinal, or ecclesiastical margins. Indeed, the church of Jesus Christ was barely underway when the marginalized ones took the stage. In Mark's Gospel the Apostle John says to Jesus, "Teacher, we saw someone casting out demons in your name, and we tried to stop him, because he was not following us." To which Jesus responds, "Do not stop him; for no one who does a deed of power in my name will be able soon afterward to speak evil of me. Whoever is not against us is for us" (Mark 9:38–40). In Acts 8 we are introduced to the saga of a magician named Simon, aka "the Great," who believed and was baptized through the witness of the Apostle Philip. Amazed by the apostolic miracles he observed, and associating that power with the ritual of the laying on of hands, Simon attempted to purchase the power of the Holy Spirit, only to receive this curt response from the Apostle Peter: "May your silver perish with you, because you thought you could obtain God's gift with money." Peter urged Simon to repent and avoid divine judgment for his materialistic mistake (Acts 8:9–24). Simon did not fare well in this world if not the next. His name was later morphed into the word *simony*, a derisive term for the buying and selling of church offices.

And that was only the beginning. From the first-century efforts of Simon the Great to the third-century Montanists, to twenty-first-century Appalachian serpent handlers, Christian history is replete with marginalized believers, intentionally outside or judged to be outside the boundaries of doctrinal and ecclesiastical convention. Some remain the unreconciled heretics or charlatans, ever on the theological outskirts of the church, while others of the marginalized turn out to be the forebears of tomorrow's orthodoxy. No *guide* to the church's history can ignore those people and movements, focusing on their beliefs, and listening, where possible, to their elusive, sometimes neglected voices as understood or interpreted by the guardians of order and orthodoxy.

These days I often feel cross-pulled between the tug of tradition and the pull of the margins. Perhaps the tension is good and the feast is a moveable one.

THE BISHOP

## The Church's Story: The Irony of It All

This pursuit of Christianity on the margins is in no way definitive. Rather, it offers an illustrative approach to the elusive nature of orthodoxy; the diversity of biblical and theological interpretations; the appearance of strange, new revelations; the power and unpredictability of prophets; and the irony of it all. Of course the Christian gospel is serious, intense, and meaningful. Martyrdom is no laughing matter. The Jesus Story chronicles words and experiences of life and death, brokenness and transformation, time and eternity. Indeed, such gospel-intensity is illustrated, often at fever pitch, by many of the marginalized movements discussed here. But while the gospel may be deadly serious, we who pursue it need not always take ourselves too seriously, making room for at least a modicum of humility in even our most provocative moments of "enthusiastical" religion.

Nor should we romanticize the marginal ones as simply misunderstood or misinterpreted. Many were quite intentional in their decision to be and remain outside the sphere of theological normalcy. Some were religious geniuses; others were simply crazy; knowing which is witch is a great challenge and at times completely fascinating. Through it all, exploring the gospel margins reminds us that we are all orthodox or heretical, mainline or marginalized, a little or a lot, affected by persons and ideas recognized and unrecognized, implicit and explicit, and situated inside or outside the church.

We are, in Frederick Buechner's words, "a family plot," given to assorted spiritual and cultural DNAs. Reflecting on that, Buechner writes: "I am necropolis. Fathers and mothers, brothers and cousins and uncles, teachers, lovers, friends, all these invisibles manifest themselves in my visibleness. Their voices speak in me, and I catch myself sometimes speaking in their voices."[3] There are even times when we cannot call our motives and mentors by name they are tucked so deeply inside us, stuck there by God knows who or God knows where, but carrying us toward the spiritual or ecclesiastical status quo or away from it, often at breakneck speed. That's the irony of it all; when the things we thought would never save us do, and the things we thought would save us can't. We are, as Paul says, "earthen vessels," given to numerous missteps and malapropisms in our efforts to articulate and live out God's good news. Recognizing the ironic is a way of sustaining us when the journey itself is long and hard, and we are not so sure about the route we have taken.

Sometimes I think that besides Jesus, one of the major reasons I relish the Christian gospel is the irony of it all. To open the pages of Holy Scripture or to read the history of the church is to come to terms with the amazing irony of Divine grace. What is irony, after all? Official definitions are readily available and, in this case, quite provocative.

There is a certain grace to letting those that have gone before us live in their time with all their dignities and disasters. Surely our own earthiness will be clear to our heirs a hundred years from now.

**THE ELDER**

Irony, says the *American Heritage Dictionary*, is the "incongruity between what might be expected and what actually occurs."[4] And isn't that idea strangely comparable to another definition, this one in the book of Hebrews as translated in the *New English Bible*: "Faith gives substance to our hopes, and makes us certain of realities we do not see" (Hebrews 11:1). Faith makes us certain of realities we do not see, it involves (dare we say it) "the incongruity between what might be expected and what actually occurs."

We have only to read the New Testament to realize that in the Jesus Story, faith and irony get all mixed up together. It begins that way. An angel announces to a virgin named Mary that she will bear "the Son of the most High." Then she visits her cousin Elizabeth who as it turns out is also pregnant after having been long labeled with that terrible biblical word, "barren," and it's all so wild and joyous that whenever Mary walks past Elizabeth's belly, John the Baptist kicks the daylights out of his mother's tummy. Did both those women laugh or at least chuckle a little at the incongruity of their situations? And, as if that weren't enough, Mary sings about all that in an ironic little song—half praise chorus, half socio-economic manifesto:

> Tell out my soul the greatness of the Lord, rejoice, rejoice, my spirit in God my Saviour; so tenderly has he looked upon his servant, humble as she is . . . the arrogant of heart and mind he has banished, he has torn imperial powers from their thrones, but the humble have been lifted high. The hungry he has satisfied with good things, the rich sent away empty. (Luke 1:26–56 NEB)

Irony is compounded when Mary's son, a Nazarene carpenter, manufactures 180 gallons of vintage wine in the twinkling of an eye and the Gospel of John says this was "the first of the signs by which he revealed his glory and led his disciples to believe in him" (John 2:1–11). Later, someone asks Jesus, "Who is my neighbor?" and he tells the story of a good Samaritan, a man tainted with bad blood, the worst possible hero in first-century Judea. And when someone else asks him about the Kingdom of God and Jesus says, (ironically) that in God's New Day (aka "the Kingdom") the workers who show up at quitting time get the same wages as the workers who've been working since dawn. (I hate that story. I also love that story, since I'm never sure what crowd I'm in.) And in the greatest Irony of all (Paul calls it "foolishness"), the church declares that Jesus's own death on a Roman cross was an event with salvific—great word, *salvific*—even cosmic, implications that changed the world forever. Perhaps the resurrection of Jesus Christ, like no other event in the church's history, illustrates ultimate irony, "the incongruity between what might be expected and what actually occurs."

## History and Myth: Retelling the Jesus Story

A *guide* to the *history of the church* must also explore the nature of history itself, and the various ways in which historical material is written and understood, interpreted and misunderstood. To understand something of the Jesus Story and its impact on the continuing history of Christianity, we must begin with history as *actual event*, the appearance at a particular moment in time of a man we know as Jesus of Nazareth who became to the church, Jesus the Christ. His birth is dated at around 6–4 BCE, based on the historical rule of Herod the Great. He was born in Bethlehem, but reared in Nazareth in the Galilee.

Jesus was Jewish! No, really, studies show! He inherited an entire religious tradition and context that shaped his understanding of the God of Abraham, Isaac, Jacob, and Moses; a ritual related to the sacrificial system of the Temple in Jerusalem and the worship/communal setting of synagogue; a written authority including Torah, Psalms, and Prophets; and a linguistic heritage of people's Aramaic, synagogue Hebrew, and perhaps a little Latin because Rome ruled the world, Nazareth included. To tell and retell the Jesus Story required the church to know, or at least deal with, the cultural, religious, ethnic, and personal context into which Jesus came. The Jesus Story begins with an actual event, the birth of Jesus at a specific point in time.

*Actual events* are of course the stuff of history. Early martyrs die under years of Roman persecution;

Constantine wins the battle of Milvan Bridge in 312; St. Anthony goes into the desert to purify his soul and lives to be 105; Rome is conquered in 410; St. Augustine sends his nameless mistress and mother of their child packing after fifteen years together; the Council of Nicaea rules against Arius in 325; Pope Innocent III instigates a crusade against the Cathari in 1208, and approves the Franciscan Order in 1215; Martin Luther nails Ninety-Five Theses to the door of the Castle Church in Wittenberg in 1517; and so it goes. But we know about those events, not because we were there, but because they have been described for us.

So the retelling of the Jesus Story and the church's history also involves history as *described event* recounted for us by actual witnesses, or by those who related details through oral or written history. *Described history* provides certain details, while no doubt omitting others. So in a sense, it is often possible that the people who describe historical events may also control them, implicitly if not outright.

This means that history as *described event* is closely related to history as *interpreted event*, since every recounting carries some sort of interpretation given the way events are detailed. Nowhere is this more evident than in the meaning that is given to Jesus's life, death, resurrection, and the community of those who for varying reasons took the name Christian to identify themselves with him. It is in history as *interpreted event* that the Jesus Story moves across two centuries with multiple versions of who he was, what his teachings meant, and how his ideas are to be expressed in the community of the church.

Even the Gospels begin at different segments of his life, offering diverse introductions/interpretations to what his appearance meant. Mark, the first of the Gospels, omits any reference to Jesus's origins, and begins with God's anointing of him at his baptism in River Jordan. Matthew gives him a very Jewish lineage with a DNA stretching all the way back to Abraham. Matthew details the saga of Jesus's birth with a multicultural recognition by the Magi/astrologers, a paranoid dictator (Herod), and a rapid exile in Egypt (the Holy Family as illegal aliens?). Luke offers the most extensive infancy narrative, beginning with that wonderful theological/historical phrase: "And it came to pass in those days . . ." (Luke 2:1 KJV), and the Christmas nativity scene begins. By the time John's Gospel appears on the scene in the early second century, Jesus's birth has taken on cosmic implications, with another historical/theological *interpretation* altogether: "In the beginning was the Word, and the Word was with God, and the Word was God" (John 1:1). The infant refugee has become the very *Logos* of God; "the true light, which enlightens everyone," had come into the world (John 1:9).

By the time the Apostle Paul shows up, the man from Nazareth is interpreted accordingly: "God was in Christ, reconciling the world" (2 Corinthians 5:19). Yet not everyone was sold. Indeed, Tacitus, the Roman historian, reports Jesus's crucifixion by Pontius Pilate, then adds: "Checked for the moment, this pernicious superstition again broke out, not only in Judaea, the source of the evil, but even in Rome, that receptacle for everything that is sordid and degrading. . . ."[5]

Some two millennia later, another doubter, Christopher Hitchens, would write: "There were many deranged prophets roaming Palestine at the time, but this one [Jesus] reportedly believed himself, at least some of the time, to be god or the son of god." Hitchens concludes that, "Either the Gospels are in some sense literal truth, or the whole thing is essentially a fraud and perhaps an immoral one at that."[6] In one sense, the history of the Christian church is one long illustration of history as *interpreted event*, from ardent believers to ardent skeptics to ardent antagonists. Critiques of Jesus and the Jesus Story have been present since the church began.

---

**THE DEACON**

Does the fact that for the Christian it is not just history that is being interpreted, but ourselves and God make this conversation much more difficult in a secular public square?

---

Sometimes the Jesus Story is captivated by *popular recollection*, a culture-wide engagement with various elements of the Story in the imagination or tradition of an entire society, or at least significant elements thereof. The Christmas celebration is perhaps the most global illustration of the impact of Christian influence on *popular recollection.* Throughout the world, individuals inside and outside the church give some attention to Christmas in serious participation in Advent, Christmas Eve, and other Christmas observances, while others use it as an occasion for gift-giving or other Christmas-related observances, a long way from any specific faith. The concern of many conservatives that shop clerks no longer wish them

"Merry Christmas" when taking their money at shopping malls and other temples of mammon illustrate the way in which a specific event described and interpreted within the Christian community has been co-opted in the culture to such an extent that its theological *interpretation* is inseparable from the *popular recollection* of an entire culture.

## The Church and Myth: The World We are Born into and the World Born into Us

To reflect on history as *popular recollection* is to examine the relationship between church and culture in Christian history. Clifford Geertz suggests that culture "denotes an historically transmitted pattern of meanings embodied in symbols, a system of inherited concepts expressed in symbolic forms by means of which . . . [individuals] communicate, perpetuate, and develop their knowledge about and attitudes toward life."[7] In other words, cultures pass on values, rituals, and identity though myths, sources of identity for individuals or groups. The details of the myth do not have to be factual for the myth to be true, though it is an effective way of providing identity. Mark Shorer describes myth as "a large controlling image that gives philosophical meaning to the facts of ordinary life; that is, which has organizing value for experience."[8]

---

In preacher speak, *never let the truth get in the way of a good story.*

THE BISHOP

---

America as a "Christian nation" is one illustration of the power of myth in a specific culture. It continues to find its way into public discourse, creating debates as to the religious orientation of the colonial founders: Were they evangelicals, deists, or dissenters? Did they intend for Christianity to be the religious and moral center of the nation? While there are clearly religious overtones to the idea, the facts suggest that the First Amendment to the U.S. Constitution opened the door to religious pluralism, which has steadily evolved to include Protestant sects—Baptists, Quakers, Pentecostals—to new movements such as Mormons, Christian Scientists, Jehovah's Witnesses, Scientologists—to non-Christian traditions that include Native Americans, Jews, Muslims, Buddhists, and others. By the twenty-first century, a growing number of persons in the U.S. increasingly exercise their First Amendment rights to claim no religious commitments at all. Sorting out the myth of American religious identity remains a work in progress.

Myths are essential for individual and collective identity. Sometimes the myth holds and sometimes it does not. Sorting all that out is one of the great adventures and challenges of the study of Christian history. Rollo May sums up the power and the dangers of myths as sources of identity: "Thus true myths and symbols, so long as they retain their original power always carry an element of ultimate meaning which illuminates but reaches beyond each [individual's] concrete experience." He concludes, "When a myth loses its power to demand some stand from us, it has become only a tale."[9]

What do we do with those crazy stories about St. Francis talking to the wolves? Can they be a tale for me but a myth to my Catholic neighbor?

THE ELDER

## Things Change—They Remain the Same

Myth and story, text and tradition have shaped the church from its origins to the present day. While some issues and ideas, beliefs and practices come and go, new approaches to the Christian gospel appear with great regularity, often as those on the margins challenge or replace ecclesiastical leaders and establishments. Nonetheless, in every age, the church responds to issues, ideas that were present from the beginning or almost. The approaches and dogmas associated with those ideas create both unity and division; they provoke great treatises and continuing exploration by clergy and laity, in the pulpit and the pew. Some of those ideas and issues are discussed in this brief *Guide to Church History*.

- And, believe it or not, all this brings us back to the serpent handlers. In ways I still can't explain, my encounter with them taught me something about the nature of the church and the continuing questions that haunt the Communion of Saints from beginning to end. That realization began for me some six to eight months after my initial visit to the outdoor serpent handling, and on the occasion of the visit of Brother Arnold Saylor to my class at the Baptist seminary in Louisville. Saylor had never been on a seminary campus before and he kept pressing me as to why preachers who were truly called thought they should go to school to learn how to do it. When class started Saylor was very nervous and literally put himself against the wall at the head of the class.

- Students, especially some who considered themselves biblical inerrantists, pressed him on the question of BIBLICAL AUTHORITY and how he could be so literal about the "taking up serpents" and drinking "an unclean thing" and not be harmed. Saylor simply took their form of biblical literalism and turned it back on them. The text is clear, he told them; such miraculous signs "follow them that believe" and are essential for "confirming the word of God." Indeed, he reminded them that in the Mark 16 passage, "Jesus is the one doing the talking." And by the time he finished his biblical exegesis, Brother Saylor was roaming the front of the class and the students were the ones who had their backs to the wall! He taught me this: be careful how you hold to biblical authority. It may force you into places you'd rather not go!
- Serpent handlers also taught me about the power of oral tradition in shaping Christian worship, indeed, identity, then and now. Saylor told my class

that he fought the call to preach largely because he was semi-literate; he couldn't read well. He told them that if they should write him a letter (this was pre-email) his wife would have to read it to him. But when he "answered the call," he found he could read the Bible and that was a confirmation of his decision! Hearing him that day, and in serpent-handling worship services, it seemed to me that he had memorized long passages from the King James Version of the Bible as he heard them in his own Pentecostal-Holiness community, a firsthand reminder of how the Bible (and the church) came into being. Retelling the Jesus Story in its many voices and versions is essential and unending in the life of the church.

- The serpent handlers also compelled me to reflect on the power and presence of the church's worship as I had never considered it before. Like many mountain Christians, they baptize by immersion, wash feet, and share the Lord's Supper with bits of unleavened bread and shot glasses full of temperance grape juice. In a real sense, however, their serpent handling suggests that the sacrament is alive and it can kill you, and every time you come to worship it is a matter of life and death.

I'm no serpent handler, let me make that clear, but worship with them was a powerful reminder that immersion baptism (in my own Baptist tradition) speaks of death, burial, resurrection—transformational danger. And that the words at Christ's Table about body and blood, life and death are themselves equally dangerous and grace giving.

Strange that a small, rather bizarre Appalachian sect would capture my own attention regarding the nature of Christian experience and identity with or without rattlesnakes. "Remember, Lord, your church," the writer of the *Didache* chanted. "Save it from all evil and make it perfect in your love, and gather it together in its holiness from the four winds, into your kingdom which you have prepared for it."[10] Perhaps this *guide* is simply one attempt to discern certain clues for remembering the church, in its high moments of love and holiness, and in certain low moments when evil got the best of it. The church is where the Spirit is. But discerning the Spirit is not always easy. Ironic, isn't it?

# 2

# Who's in Charge around Here?

*"About apostles and prophets, follow the rule of the Gospel, which is this: Let every apostle who comes to you be welcomed as the Lord. But he shall not stay more than one day, and if it is necessary the next day also. But if he stays three days, he is a false prophet."*[1]

Didache

So the Didache, an early manual on church order written around 110 CE, advises fledgling Christian congregations on what to do when the traveling preachers come to town. Then as now, determining who is and isn't a prophet is not easy. As the *Didache* tells it, best to welcome them all as you would the Lord. But since some prophets actually weren't that at all, best to let them do their thing and then move them along. Two days tops! Three-day prophets can get you into all kinds of trouble.

It was a simple formula for a complex issue of spiritual discernment. From the very start, issues of church authority could stabilize the church, and split it wide open. It's not gotten any easier after 2,000 years. In fact, one of the church's greatest and perhaps most divisive questions is: Who's in charge? Where does apostolic authority rest in the body of Christ? The means for authenticating church leaders is as intricate and challenging now as it was when the church was brand new.

---

THE DEACON

I was told growing up if a prophet preaches, angels sprinkle gold dust from on high. Not joking, Mainliners.

---

## "With the Laying on of Hands"

On June 20, 1971, I was ordained to the Gospel Ministry, so the ordination certificate reads to this day. I reread it from time to time, still wondering what in the world it means to be a gospel minister. The ordination took place in Texas, at the Northridge Baptist Church in Mesquite, a suburb of Dallas. My church history professor, William R. Estep, drove the forty-five miles from Southwestern Baptist Theological Seminary in Fort Worth to preach the ordination sermon. Those were the old days when students held professors in awe (studies show), and I was terribly pleased that Dr. Estep, a faithful mentor, had consented to lead the service. At the ordaining council he asked me a question and I stumbled, as I recall. For the life of me I can't remember the question, but I have a distinct memory of choking in his presence, a bit of vanity and humiliation that I carry to this day. But I passed—I wonder if I still would—and they ordained me. The service was simple and to the point, like Dr. Estep's sermon. I recall little that was said, but have profound memories of that unspoken ritual, the laying on of hands, a symbolic act that has acquired sacramental implications in my life.

Those people trusted God and the future enough to take a chance on me as a minister. It was a gamble, to be sure—I'm guessing that a few of them had reservations. After all, I was a child of the 1960s, and the fact that the first sermon series I ever preached, at the church's youth revival, had titles taken from Beatles' songs—I blush to tell this—was a little too worldly for some of those Texas Baptists. But if they were worried, they kept it to themselves. (The sermons were horrible, by the way.) When it was time for laying on hands, that ancient practice passed on from the book of Acts, I remember the people trooping by, placing hands on my head; caring hands of good Baptist people, burning some gospel into me with a rite I still find powerful and mysterious.

What did it mean, that ordination now decades old? Did it convey some supernatural authority by which other Christian brothers and sisters are brought into submission to some autocratic under-shepherd? Not for a moment. Did it create some special status that qualifies me for assorted ministerial authority in church and culture? Sometimes, but not always. Decades after those hands were laid on me, I'm still sorting out what it means to be a Reverend, or whether it means much of anything at all.

## Where Do Leaders Come From? Apostolic Credentials and Credentialing

"Gifts" and/or specific interchurch functions appeared quickly among the first Christian congregations. These functions are listed by the Apostle Paul (a rather questionable title, early on) in his letter to the Corinthians: "Within our community God has appointed, in the first place apostles, in the second place prophets, thirdly teachers; then miracle-workers, then those who have gifts of healing, or ability to help others or power to guide them, or the gift of ecstatic utterance of various kinds." (1 Corinthians 12:28—This text from the New English Bible raises the possibility of a church full of "ecstatic utterers"!)

For the first Christians, apostolic authority was central to the church's identity, as close as they could get to Christ's vision for the New Covenant. And since many believed that Christ's return was just around the corner, it sometimes appeared as if apostolic teaching would carry the church until God's New Day came roaring in. The Twelve were Jesus's closest associates, the ones to whom he gave direct instruction, beyond all those nebulous parables he offered everyone else. (When Judas betrayed Jesus and then did himself in, the remaining eleven "cast lots," securing a new colleague named Matthias. Paul, however, seems to have secured Divine credentialing.)

By the time of Paul's first letter to Corinth, the fledgling churches already recognized an array of individuals who manifested a variety of specific gifts within the community of faith. It is a list reflecting something of a first-century hierarchy, first, second, third, etc., all the way down to ecstatic utterers (tongue-talkers). In one sense, baptism was the great equalizer, abolishing hierarchies in religion and culture. In another sense, however, the church quickly acknowledged the necessity for persons whose "calling" was to preach the gospel, administer the sacraments of baptism and the Lord's Supper, and provide pastoral care for the new people of God.

---

**THE DEACON**

Baptism, the Table, and speaking in tongues seem to be multipurposed for both equalizing and dividing depending on the tradition. I am guessing that it's hard to make a power grab while foot-washing.

---

But barely a letter later (2 Corinthians) Paul is already hedging his bets on apostolic authority, contrasting his own apostolic CV with that of a crowd he calls the "super-apostles," aka "false apostles, deceitful workers, disguising themselves as apostles of Christ" (2 Corinthians 11:5, 13). Paul, née Saul, former public enemy of the Jesus People, had difficulty convincing them that he was really one of them, and thus was forced to include his resumé in almost every letter he wrote. And discerning the proper ecclesiastical authorities didn't get any easier as the church expanded.

## Traveling Prophets and Settled Pastors

In fact, one of the first genuine splits in early Christian churches blew up almost immediately over which crowd was most authoritative, the traveling prophets who moved from house-church to house-church exercising their charismatic gifts of direction and declaration, or the growing number of settled presbyters who were chosen by congregations and put down roots in the local communities. These offices reflect particular responses to the spiritual and practical needs of the earliest Christian communities. Early on, the terms *bishop*, *presbyter* (priest), and *elder* were used interchangeably for those functioning in the pastoral office. Deacons were responsible for the collection and dispersion of church funds, particularly in response to persons in dire straits.

Predictably, controversies soon developed over which prophets and what teachings the churches should follow. By the early second century, things got so bad at the ever-dysfunctional churches in Corinth that Clement, bishop of the church in Rome, felt obligated to intervene. Problems apparently arose when a group of traveling prophets showed up in Corinth and convinced some of the church members to reject the local recognized ministers in favor of the revelations of the charismatic visitors. It was not pretty. In a letter dated around 95 CE, Clement attempted to set things straight. In doing so he articulated perhaps the earliest and certainly one of the most basic explanations of what became the idea of apostolic authority in the church.

---

THE BISHOP

Thinking of just how early the church started splitting into new churches I am amazed it took so long for a Reformation and just how surprised people are when it happens today. Maybe church splits are in the DNA and help the church innovate and keep moving? I still prefer the Book of Common Prayer.

---

## Apostolic Authority: Jesus's Leadership Plan?

Clement's suggested formula for dealing with contradictory (and contrary) prophets and apostles went like this: "The apostles received the gospel for us from the Lord Jesus Christ; Jesus the Christ was sent from God. So Christ is from God, and the apostles from Christ. . . . So as [the apostles] preached . . . they appointed their first converts, after testing them by the Spirit, as superintendents and assistants of those who were to believe."[2] In other words, Jesus was the ultimate fulfillment of God's word; he called and taught a special group of apostles, giving them authority to tell the story and sending them out; they in turn appointed others to perpetuate the gospel truth. Thus their teaching charted the church's course, and its authority could be traced all the way back to Jesus.

Apostolic teaching and authority seemed relatively secure when the churches were small and when Jesus's return seemed imminent. But when Jesus tarried, his larger plan went into effect, Clement said, since the Savior knew "that there would be contention for the title of overseer." (Does nothing change in the church?)

---

**THE ELDER**

I am waiting for you to say Jesus established the first church committee and called for a Capital Campaign.

---

Thus the apostles instructed and appointed certain ecclesiastical authorities "in order that if they should fall asleep [meaning die], other approved men should succeed to their duties." As Clement saw it, the Corinthian Christians were on the right track when they appointed such "reputable men, with the consent of the whole church," who would serve Christ's flock "humbly, quietly, and disinterestedly." But certain false prophets had cast their spell, and the duly elected, trusted leaders were "unjustly removed from their ministry."[3] Clement urged their restoration by the authority of Jesus Christ. Debates over the nature of apostolic teaching and authority began early in the church's history. Questions immediately arose over where the correct doctrine was to be found and who had the proper spiritual and apostolic credentials to lead churches.

## The Bishop Is "As the Lord"—Normative Authority in Motion

By the second and third centuries, such credentialing had become more specific and systematic. A threefold hierarchy included bishops, presbyter/elders, and deacons. The one church in a given location—Antioch, Ephesus, Rome, etc.—was actually a collection of multiple house communities. With time, and for the sake of unity (and of course power), certain leading individuals of sterling character, pastoral experience, and courage in the face of persecution, rose to leadership and became known as bishops, the direct spiritual and doctrinal descendants of the Apostles. They were charged with caring for the flock of God.

Bishops became the chief spiritual leaders through whom correct doctrine and practice was transmitted. Presbyters or elders (an often interchangeable designation) were the primary pastoral figures in the various churches—preaching, offering the sacraments, providing the care of souls; while deacons were those who saw to the physical needs of the faithful and had responsibility for church funds. The bishop's presence was required for baptisms and ordinations, and they represented the

Christ-centered, Christ-related connection to the church's origins.

---

**THE BISHOP**

I may have some authority, but Jesus would have just as much trouble as I when it comes to herding cats! PS: that's how bishops talk about the laity when you aren't around.

---

Church teaching increasingly emphasized that the bishop was "as the Lord," around whom the people of God are to gather. In his letter to the Trallians (don't worry, I'm a professor and I'd never heard of them either), Ignatius, the bishop of Antioch wrote:

> For when you subordinate yourselves to the bishop as to Jesus Christ you appear to me to be living not in a human way, but after the manner of Jesus Christ. . . . It is necessary, therefore . . . that you do nothing without the bishop, but subordinate yourselves also to the board of elders as to the apostles of Jesus Christ our hope. . . . And the deacons too, as ministers of the mysteries of Jesus Christ, must please all in every way.[4]

In his letter to the Smyrnaeans (same here), Ignatius was even more direct, declaring that nothing related to the work and beliefs of the church could be done without the bishop. He concluded: "Wherever the bishop appears, let the people be, just as wherever Jesus Christ is, there is the universal [catholic] church. It is not permissible to baptize or hold a religious meal [Eucharist] without the bishop, but whatever he approves is also pleasing to God, so that everything you do may be secure and valid."[5] Christ's authority was thus inseparable from the office and person of the bishop throughout the whole church.

---

Not to be rude, but doesn't this seem like the people are outsourcing their responsibility as disciples to the bishop? Jesus seemed to be confident when empowering and sending his peeps out.

**THE ACOLYTE**

---

## What Happens When the Bishop Goes Bad?

The early Christians—at least many of them—came to believe that the true teaching of the church was passed on from Jesus to the Apostles, to those taught by the Apostles, or those taught by the people who had been taught by the apostles, and on down the line. Roman Catholic, Eastern Orthodox, and Anglican Christians are among those who continue that tradition, called "apostolic succession." The bishop was the central agent in assuring the people of God that they remained on the right track in doctrine and practice. But, what happens when the bishop goes bad and leads the church astray? It was bound to happen.

In the early fourth century, for example, the Roman Emperor Diocletian instituted a period of persecution against Christians, demanding that they offer sacrifices to the cult of the emperor as a sign of their good citizenship and shared spirituality with other Roman subjects. The persecution even involved confiscation and burning of Christian sacred writings. Apparently, some bishops participated by turning over holy texts. When the persecution ended, questions arose about the continued authority of those book-burning bishops.

A group of purists identified with a rigorist bishop named Donatus (we know them as Donatists) turned apostolic succession back on itself, suggesting that those who had been ordained or baptized by those who had been ordained or baptized by the apostate bishops had to do it all over again with a more spiritually uncorrupted successor of Jesus Christ. Thus the question: *Does the character of the administrator determine the validity of the sacrament?* Is Christ's presence tainted by the immorality of Christ's representative? And, is that betrayal passed on through a kind of cruel misdirection of grace? The Donatists argued that the only redemption possible to the spiritual traitors was found in repentance and rebaptism. Easy absolution by a priest or bishop was cheap grace. This turmoil produced serious divisions and varied remedies.

---

I think post-social media it would be impossible to think the one presiding over a sacrament determined its efficacy. Once parents and professors were added to Facebook I had some serious evidence of "backsliding" to delete.

**THE DEACON**

---

## When the Bishop Goes Bad: Multiple Remedies

### *Remedy I: Rebaptism*

The problem of episcopal corruption, morally or doctrinally, was a major issue in the early church. Some believed that the authority of Christ enabled the bishop to "bind and loose"—that is, excommunicate or absolve—persons on earth and in heaven. Absolution and restoration were possible through apostolic authority alone. The Donatists, among others, disagreed. Christians who had sinned after baptism were in serious jeopardy, particularly after the most heinous sins of adultery, apostasy, or murder. The only solution was for the apostates to throw themselves on God's mercy and live a life of penance. Rebaptism would help if anything could.

THE DEACON

This theory is still in use at many summer youth camps, but mostly as a means to deal with cursing, role-playing games, heavy petting, and thinking about heavy petting.

### *Remedy II: Councils of Bishops*

Bishops could go astray, so the church would do well to trust that the Holy Spirit spoke best through councils of bishops, gathered to decide on crucial questions facing the church at large. When bishops differed, or when certain bishops compromised their moral or doctrinal authority, it fell to the bishops from the *oikoumene*, "the whole inhabited world," to set things straight. Bishops came together at regional synods, and ultimately, *ecumenical* councils for the whole church. Majority vote of the bishops at Nicaea in 325 CE, the church's first great ecumenical council, affirmed the Trinity and that the Father and the Son were "of the same substance" in their deity. It set the precedent for further councils, a lineage Orthodox churches trace to the first seven gatherings, and Roman Catholics trace to the Second Vatican Council in the 1960s.

But what happens when councils of bishops contradict each other? The Council of Ephesus was called by another emperor in 431 to deal with a controversy over the divine/human natures of Christ. Cyril, the bishop of Alexandria, stressed the unity of humanity and divinity in the Christ, stressing divinity as the means for redeeming the human race. Nestorius, the patriarch of Constantinople, insisted that Christ's humanity and divinity were less a unity than a "conjunction," with his fully human nature (he is, after all, the "second Adam") necessary to redeem sinful humanity.

Historian W. H. C. Frend describes Nestorius as not simply "loquacious and tactless but also limited as a theologian." Cyril, however, was a real piece of work, whom Frend calls complicit in the murder of an ecclesiastical colleague, mean-spirited in his treatment of other church leaders, and "unscrupulous . . . in his use of bribes to gain his ends."[6]

In response, Theodosius II, the Roman Emperor, called the Ephesus Council. Cyril and his supporters were the first to show up, with some two hundred other bishops who joined him in denouncing Nestorius and declaring him deposed from his post in Constantinople. Then they went home, heresy overcome, no muss no fuss. But four days later, John, the bishop of Antioch, arrived with forty-three bishops who joined him in ordering Cyril deposed and promoting Nestorius's views of Christ's nature.[7] Where in the world was the Holy Spirit, and which group of apostolic successors had the truth? Ultimately Emperor Theodosius took matters into his own hands, deposed Nestorius and ruled in favor of Cyril and his "two-nature" theory of Christ's humanity and divinity. This would have happened, Professor Frend observes, even "without Cyril's massive bribes at the imperial court."[8] Apparently, if the Holy Spirit didn't speak best through councils of bishops, a little money would do the trick anyway.

THE BISHOP

I can't decide if this sounds exciting because key doctrines were being debated or that theological opponents had such cool names back then.

### *Remedy III: The Bishop of Rome, a Pope for All Seasons*

When all else fails, when bishops contradict each other and when church councils crash and burn, many looked to the one bishop who represented consistency and stability (at least most of the time): the Bishop of Rome, aka the pope. For the first three Christian centuries, Rome was the center of the universe, the source of kingdom, power, and glory.

For Christians, Rome was the site of the "double apostolicity," the place where Peter and Paul were martyred. Peter himself was thought to be the first bishop of the church at Rome, and he was perceived by many as the source of church authority received directly from Christ, as set forth in Matthew: "You are Peter, and upon this rock I will build my church and the gates of hell shall not prevail against you. And I will give to you the keys of the kingdom of heaven and whatever you bind on earth will be bound in heaven; and whatever you loose on earth will be loosed in heaven."

The reasoning went something like this: Peter is the rock on which Christ built his church. Peter was the bishop of Rome; Peter and his successors had the power of "binding and loosing" in this world and the next. They were the agents of salvation and damnation.

Such an idea took a while to take root. True enough, Rome was a central place, but with the division of the Roman Empire into eastern and western segments during the fourth century, the imperial court moved to Constantinople and a power vacuum developed in the West. Various popes attempted to fill it.

Over time, a variety of Christian leaders and writers offered deference to the Roman bishop and his place as a source of doctrinal orthodoxy, ecclesiastical authority, and political power inside and outside the church. In his third-century *Ecclesiastical History*, Eusebius of Caesarea wrote of the centrality of Rome for Christians: "Thus, then, was this man [Nero] heralded as above all the first fighter against God, and was raised up to slaughter the Apostles. It is recorded that Paul was beheaded in Rome itself and that Peter also was crucified in Nero's time, and the title of 'Peter and Paul' over the cemeteries there, which has prevailed to the present day, confirms the story."[9]

The bishop of Rome, the pope of the Roman Catholic Church, is the most enduring office, role, and institution in the history of Christianity. It evolved over multiple centuries from Pope Leo I's fifth-century assertion that he was the Vicar of St. Peter (Peter's representative on earth), to Innocent III's insistence that he was the Vicar of Christ on earth, a title that popes claim to this day.

THE ACOLYTE

Did St. Peter have those sweet ruby red pope slippers or the fancy headgear?

Catholics believe that all Roman bishops sit where Peter sat, receiving from Christ the "power of the keys" passed on across the centuries. To achieve this authority, popes utilized a succession of documents, forged and authentic; they secured military alliances with certain European monarchies; and they appointed (or tried to) bishops in countries throughout Europe. Medieval popes held office like medieval monarchs, controlling territory, hiring mercenary troops (i.e., the Swiss Guard), and installing and deposing European rulers when the prerogatives of church or pope seemed threatened. All this reached a medieval pinnacle in the thirteenth-century with Boniface VIII, who declared that the pope had control over both the two great swords of authority of church and state: faith and order in this world and the next.

## Protestants and Church Authority: Bishops, Presbyteries, Congregations, and the Holy Ghost

After Martin Luther posted his 95 Theses criticizing the selling of indulgences and challenging papal authority, Pope Leo X dismissed the document as the ravings of a drunken monk who would change his tune once he sobered up. When Luther didn't, the pope threatened excommunication in a papal bull (meaning declaration) that began "Arise O Lord and judge thy cause, a wild boar is loose in thy vineyard." Luther and his students burned the bull in the streets of Wittenberg, the pope excommunicated him, and the Protestant Reformation was underway. Luther labeled the pope the Antichrist, and the conversation went downhill from there, including this little ditty: "May God punish you, I say, you shameless, barefaced liar, devil's mouthpiece, who dares to spit out, before God, before all the angels, before the dear sun, before all the world, your devil's filth."[10] The pope was not pleased. It was not a pretty parting of the ways.

Martin Luther re-formed an understanding of the nature of ordination and calling as sources of authority in the church. First, he said, quoting Paul, "The just shall live by faith" (Romans 1:17). Sinners may go directly to God through Christ to exercise and experience salvation by faith, without the intercession of a special clergy-class. He cut out the middle man. This idea came to be known as the priesthood of all believers. Second, Luther refused to distinguish between callings or vocations. The Christian priesthood was no more special than the mother washing dirty diapers at the sink. He wrote, "Workers with brawn are prone to despise workers with brain such as city secretaries and schoolteachers. . . . As for schoolteaching, it is so strenuous that no one ought to be bound to it for more than ten years."[11]

Yet Luther also continued the ordination of clergy, and later Lutherans even used bishops as chief ecclesiastical administrative officers. Nonetheless, Luther denied that ordination brought any special authority by which the sacraments of baptism and the Lord's Supper were validated or turned into vehicles of grace. Catholic views of ordination created "implacable discord" that made clergy and laity "separated farther than heaven and earth to the incredible injury of baptismal grace and to the confusion of evangelical fellowship."[12]

## Calvinists, Presbyterians, and Covenants

John Calvin, the reformer of Geneva, sought a biblical model for church authority, resting leadership in a fourfold set of officers: 1) Pastors offer a ministry of "word and sacrament" within the community of faith; 2) Teachers provide for the appropriate doctrinal and biblical instruction for "the flock of God";[13] 3) Deacons exercise the care of souls with particular concern for the neediest of persons; 4) and Elders see to the administration of ecclesiastical details. This group of ordained ministers (pastor, teacher, deacon) joined the elders (a lay office) in forming the presbytery, the governing regional body of the church.

## Congregationalists: The Authority of Christ through the Community of Faith

Another source of church authority came from the Congregationalists, a view of the church that grew out of seventeenth-century Puritanism and the belief that the authority of Christ is mediated through the congregation of Christian believers. The congregation thus voted on matters regarding ministry and practice. The twofold officers of the church were pastors and deacons.

Early Baptists described their congregational leaders in a confession of faith from 1611: "That the Officers of every Church or congregation are either Elders, who by their office do especially feed the flock concerning their souls . . . or Deacons, Men and Women who by their office relieve the necessities of the poor and impotent brethren concerning their bodies."[14] Congregationalists understood church leadership as chosen by God and confirmed by the congregation of the faithful.

---

When did Congregationalists like Southern Baptists manage to turn this into the Dixie-styled version of Boniface VIII?

THE ELDER

---

## The Church Is Where the Spirit Is: Authority and the Holy Ghost

When the Reformation came to Zurich in the 1520s, Ulrich Zwingli made every effort to remove all aspects of Catholicism, whitewashing the walls of the Grossmünster Cathedral to eradicate all the idolatrous frescos, getting rid of images and icons, and holding a series of disputations contrasting Catholic and Protestant dogmas. What he did not anticipate, however, was the presence of a group of young leaders to his theological left who pressed the Swiss humanist and reformer to the political and theological mandate of infant baptism for all citizens of the city. The group, known for studying the Greek New Testament with Zwingli, opted for a believers' church, with baptism administered only to those adult believers who could confess faith in Christ. At the 1523 disputation when they demanded that the Catholic mass be abolished in Zurich, Zwingli replied: "My Lords [of the city council] will decide whatever regulations are adopted in the future in regard to the Mass." In response, the radical reformer Simon Stumpf replied: "Master Ulrich, you do not have the right to place the decision on this matter in the hands of my lords, for the decision has already been made, the *Spirit of God* decides."[15] With that, the Protestant Reformation encountered one of its greatest divisions.

One continuing understanding of ecclesiastical authority in Christian history involves the presence of the Holy Spirit as the source of guidance for the community of faith. This approach suggests that authority for the church is found less in bishops, hierarchy, or other ordained offices, than in those who are aware of and "anointed" by the presence and guidance of the Holy Spirit.

As we have seen, the Montanist movement of the mid-second century was one of the early public challenges to the explicit authority of those who stood in apostolic succession. Montanus and two women, Priscilla and Maximilla, claimed the authority of the Holy Spirit beyond the leadership of bishops. Tertullian, a second-century presbyter, illustrates the divisions. Early in his ministry, Tertullian was a proponent of apostolic authority, writing that the apostles "bore witness to the faith of Christ Jesus," founding "in every city, from which other churches thereafter derived the shoot of faith and the seeds of doctrine." Thus he insisted "that if Jesus Christ sent out the Apostles to preach, no others are to be accepted as preachers but those who Christ appointed."[16] Yet when he became a Montanist some years later, Tertullian asked: "Are not we laymen priests also?" And answered, "Thus there is no bench of clergy you offer and baptize and are your own sole priest. For where there are three, there is a church, they be laymen."[17]

Spirit guidance and inspiration appeared soon enough with the Protestant Reformation, as noted in the challenge to Zwingli by Simon Stumpf and other radical reformers in Zurich. For second-generation, seventeenth-century Protestants, this reliance on the Spirit as the source of authority was particularly evident in the development of the Society of Friends (Quakers), gathered by George Fox by the 1630s. For Fox and the Quakers, all persons possessed the Inner Light of God, made known by the Holy Spirit. This Inner Light was Christ, as described in John's Gospel: "The light that enlightens everyone has come into the world." Christ the Light had only to be awakened by the Spirit's witness. And if all possessed the Light, then all, both men and women, could claim the authority of Christ to declare the gospel. Early Quaker leader Robert Barclay wrote of the "Chief Principles" of Christianity as declared by the Quakers: "therefore the testimony of the Spirit is that alone by which the true knowledge of God hath been, is and can be only revealed; . . . by the revelation of the same Spirit." Baptism and Holy Communion were valid experiences instituted by Christ, but they were founded on internal, spiritual experience, not outward forms of bread and wine. Indeed, baptism "is a pure and spiritual thing, to wit, the baptism of the Spirit and fire."[18]

Quakers went beyond Congregationalists to assert not only that the authority of Christ was mediated through the community of faith, but that the power of the inner light was so pervasive that the decisions of the Quaker meeting should be by consensus, not simple majority. Likewise, if all have the inner light, then all could preach and teach, with male and female alike as leaders of the community of faith.

**THE ELDER**

Having been at the same church for over thirty years, I can verify that there are some people in church who show no signs of an inner light.

This emphasis on the role of the Spirit in anointing church leaders was at the center of the Pentecostal movement that reasserted itself, first in the Holiness movement of the mid-nineteenth century, and then in the Pentecostal movement in the early twentieth century. Pentecostals believed that the power of the Holy Spirit fell on individuals who opened their hearts to a baptism of the Spirit, evidenced with speaking in tongues. Based on the assertion in the book of Acts that at Pentecost God's Spirit was "poured out on all flesh," then many communions allowed, indeed, encouraged women to preach. Yet they often specified that women could preach as evangelists, they could not serve as pastors, an office only permitted to males.

One of my favorite illustrations of this Spirit-led authority concerns Sister Lydia Sturgener, a Pentecostal evangelist who ran a used clothing store in Pennington Gap, Virginia in the late twentieth century. Sister Liddy discovered an abandoned church building and decided she would begin preaching in the empty building. "That church isn't dead," Sister Liddy asserted. "It's just asleep." With the help of her nephew, Junior, Sister Liddy began preaching at the deserted church. Soon others joined her and the church began to thrive. In traditional Pentecostal form, they ultimately called a male as pastor, but Sister Liddy was the real source of the church's re-formation. In many ways, the Pentecostal groups often anticipated women's leadership roles in the church, including their role as preachers and in some settings, even as duly ordained church leaders. For example, the Church of God, Cleveland, Tennessee, now not only promotes women's ordination, but recognizes their calling as pastors. More recently, however, they have restricted the office of bishop to males.

Pentecostal bishops, you say! As if to come full circle, in recent years certain Protestant churches have begun to recognize and consecrate bishops as the chief spiritual authorities in their respective communions. Some African American Pentecostals have affirmed their spiritual affinity with Coptic or Eastern Orthodox bodies, particularly united in shared concern for the experience and presence of the Holy Spirit in the lives of individuals and faith communities. Others have simply utilized the episcopal office as a means of uniting churches, affirming the Spirit's anointing, and offering authoritative guidance to churches often divided over congregational autonomy and theological differences. Nonetheless, the consecration of Pentecostal bishops is a fascinating blend of modern and ancient elements of church life.

## Authority and Office in the Church: Old Traditions, New Expressions

In some Christian traditions, the ancient idea of apostolic succession remains normative, with the episcopal office as the chief spiritual and administrative guide to the church and the faithful. Roman Catholic and Orthodox communions permit only males to serve in the office of bishop or patriarch. Both must be celibate in order to hold those offices. Both also ordain only males to the office of the priesthood; but Orthodox clergy are permitted to marry as long as they are married before the time of ordination. Roman Catholics recognize only single (celibate) males as candidates for priestly ordination. For Anglicans, some national churches such as those in England, Canada, and the U.S. permit the ordination of men and women to the priesthood and the episcopacy, while others in Africa, Asia, and South America continue to provide ordination only to males. Lutheran communions also utilize the office of bishop, some including male and female candidates. The Lutheran Church, Missouri Synod, ordains only men. So do members in good standing of the Southern Baptist Convention.

Ordination, formally executed in services involving the laying on of hands, remains a significant rite for credentialing ministerial authority figures. Who receives it, how it is administered, and what it means, continue to be questions that unite and divide the Christian church. Discerning who is a prophet and who is not remains one of the church's great challenges.

Over the years I've preached at numerous ordinations in a variety of traditions—Baptist (mostly) but also

Episcopal, Presbyterian, Moravian, and Congregational. All of those traditions let me preach; some won't let me participate in the laying on of hands, but I'm moved by them all since they offer considerable hope for the church in a new day of God's work in the world.

One of the most memorable ordinations occurred at the Wolf Creek Baptist Church, just off a county road in rural Kentucky in the 1980s. It was the ordination of Cindy Harp Johnson, one of the first ordinations of a female in which I'd ever participated. Anne Davis, my faculty colleague at the Baptist seminary in Louisville, and I were the preachers and when we came to the laying on of hands, the entire congregation was invited to participate, in keeping with the historic Baptist belief that it is the congregation that ordains through the authority of Christ passed on to the believing faith community. The members of that country church came trooping by, placing hands on Cindy's head and blessing her for the work she had done among them and would do in the larger church. Toward the end came Ms. Effie (or Ms. Ellie, I can't recall her name), the matriarch of the church, holding on to the pews as she made her way down the aisle. She pulled Cindy Harp Johnson into her considerable bosom, and in words we could all hear, blurted out, "Honey, I'm not sure where God will take you, but wherever it is, I'm for you." There was not a dry eye in the place.

Recognizing the Holy Spirit's presence is not always easy for me, but I have no doubt that the Spirit showed up at the Wolf Creek Baptist Church when Cindy Harp Johnson received the laying on of hands, and the grace of God could not be controlled.[19]

# 3

# Flaming Heretics and Anathemas Galore

*"But as for those who say, 'There was when He was not,' and, 'Before being born He was not,' and that 'He came into existence out of nothing,' or who assert that the Son of God is of a different hypostasis or substance, or created, or is subject to alteration or change—these the Catholic and apostolic Church anathematizes."*

Creed of Nicaea

In 1980, when I received tenure at the Southern Baptist Theological Seminary, in Louisville, Kentucky, I stood at the pulpit of the school's chapel and, with quill pen in hand, signed the "Abstract of Principles," the school's confessional document, in a ledger that had been signed by every tenured faculty member since the school's founding in 1859. With that signature I pledged to teach "in accordance with and not contrary to" the doctrinal statement of the Southern Baptist Convention's (SBC) oldest theological school. All went reasonably well, until the early 1990s when the seminary board of trustees, like the SBC itself, took a hard right turn theologically and ideologically.

Soon, a new set of doctrines was proposed as an addendum to the confessional mix. They were taken from a document set forth by the SBC "Peace Committee," an ad hoc group appointed to find some way through a burgeoning division in the Southern Baptist ranks. The added dogmas were to be used as guidelines for "tenure, promotion, and hiring" at the seminary. They required the following beliefs:

1. Adam and Eve were real persons.
2. The named authors did indeed write the biblical books attributed to them.
3. The miracles described in Scripture did indeed occur as supernatural events in history.
4. The historical narratives given by biblical authors are indeed accurate and reliable as given by those authors.

---

**THE ELDER**

How can Jesus be homeless when he's taken up residence in my heart?

---

For most of us faculty, it wasn't simply the dogmas but the process by which they were being imposed. We knew that once we signed off on these tenets, there would be others, until we'd either lost our theology or our souls. So we protested the changing of the rules, and the grandfathering in of new doctrinal tests for tenure and promotion. We raised concerns with our national accrediting agency, which sent a team to investigate. Ultimately, a trustee/faculty committee was established to respond to the situation, negotiating a temporary "covenant" that held long enough for a significant number of the faculty to secure other positions, leaving the seminary and its denomination to its more rightward intent. In academia, sometimes the ultimate benefit of tenure is to get you to the roof of the embassy in time to catch the last helicopter!

## *Anathema* When and Where?

The Baptist orthodoxy wars taught me this: When ideologues decide you are a heretic, they'll raise the doctrinal ante until they prove it—if not to you, at least to themselves.

---

The email Blind Carbon Copy can turn the smallest spark of doctrinal concern into a roaring fire.

**THE BISHOP**

---

Theological dictums have energized, solidified, divided, and even broken the church for 2,000 years. Sorting out true doctrine from false is no easy matter, but it remains essential, sometimes so intensely that it becomes a matter of life and death. At the same time, the history of the church reveals occasions when efforts to protect or defend against certain beliefs have fueled multiple atrocities initiated in Jesus's name, requiring repentant apologies in a later time.

That's where the word *anathema* comes in. Concluding his first letter to the Corinthians, Paul wrote, "Let anyone be accursed who has no love for the Lord. Our Lord, come!" (1 Corinthians 16:22). The Greek words *anathema* (accursed) *maranatha* (Lord, come) ultimately became watchwords for excommunication, separating unruly and/or heretical individuals not only from the church, but also from salvation itself. To provide a *guide* to *flaming heretics* requires confronting some of the church's strongest convictions and most horrendous mistakes, and searching for the wisdom to discern the difference.

Questions over the nature of Christian orthodoxy have haunted the church from the start. Very quickly multiple groups that understood themselves as Christians introduced ideas that were in conflict, even in contradiction with others. Some of those groups gained enough power, stability, and influence that their definitions of doctrine were understood as "normative," or "orthodox." Over time, they controlled the documents that defined orthodoxy itself, often undermining or even destroying alternative visions. Often in Christian history, particularly in the early centuries, we know the most about *flaming heretics* as they were articulated by the people who despised them.

In his study of *Lost Christianities*, biblical scholar Bart Ehrman notes that issues of *orthodoxy* and *heresy* once seemed clear and rather easily defined. Orthodoxy, he says, "was the right belief, taught by Jesus to his disciples and handed down by them to the leaders of the Christian churches." Heresy, on the other hand, comes "from the Greek word for 'choice,'" and refers to "intentional decisions to depart from the right belief; it implies a corruption of faith, found only among a minority of people."[1]

As his book title suggests, Ehrman insists that from the beginning there were multiple Christianities, with varying definitions of orthodoxy, ultimately defined by a "proto-orthodox" or "normative" theological majority, the ecclesiastical winners in the doctrinal wars. As thus defined, heretics were those who held false beliefs, not simply out of ignorance or from deceitful teachers, but who willfully *chose* damnable notions that carried them beyond eternal truth.[2] So *anathema* became a label applied to the excommunicated ones, often with dire spiritual, even violent, effects. Sometimes the heretics were indeed *flaming* in their obstinate insistence on alternative readings of scripture or theology. They simply would not be silent. At other times they were literally *flaming*, burned alive or otherwise executed for their perceivably false beliefs and practices.

## Gnostics: Knowing the Mysteries

One of the earliest "unorthodoxies" involved a very diverse collection of communities and individuals who were labeled *gnostic* because of their quest for secret knowledge that would bring them closer to the transcendent, unknowable God. These movements were not uniform

THE DEACON

How do we believe God worked in the history of Israel to get to Jesus and not also think the same thing about the history of "proto-orthodox" Christianity?

in their specific ideas, but developed multiple scriptures, belief systems, and eclectic ideas born of varied philosophies. Yet they shared certain parallel emphases regarding the nature of the spiritual life. For one thing, they insisted that the Source of all things, the Divine Other, was vastly separated from sinful human beings and the sinful world itself. That world was the result of creative action taken by a Demiurge, or lesser deity, whose creation is plagued by evil and suffering. Yet the transcendent, true God was made known to humans through emanations, or Aeons, spiritual beings who brought knowledge, wisdom (*Sophia*), and word (*Logos*) that provided deliverance from the evil and suffering in the world.

Gnostics believed that they understood these emanations like no one else, with a clarity of insight and vision into the secrets of the universe. The masses of human beings were trapped in the unenlightened realities of the evil, material world. For them spirit was everything, and flesh was secondary. The "god of this world," a false emanation, kept the majority of the race in ignorance and bondage.

Christian gnostics believed that Jesus was the appearance of God's greatest emanation. Yet because the flesh was

If a twenty-first-century discussion of Jesus starts out with wet dreams, then I'll stick with Science Digest.

THE ACOLYTE

a lesser state of being, Jesus only seemed to be human (a "docetic" being). His resurrected state was evidence of his full spiritual being that could appear and disappear at will, and who was not bound by material constraints, such as doors or walls. Some claimed to have received this instruction directly from Jesus by means of visions, voices, and other spiritual encounters. Others suggested that this teaching was passed on from Jesus through the Apostles and extended through later generations of gnostic teachers. Still others asserted that the true teaching was found in certain holy books that competed with what became the normative New Testament books for authority and inspiration. In various documents with varying approaches, these gnostic materials explained or illustrated the way in which the true knowledge, a source of what it meant to be truly human, was trapped in individuals but could be liberated.[3]

Leaders of "normative" Christianity did not hesitate to attack the purveyors of this secret knowledge, denouncing it as a false interpretation of Christian truth—in other words, a heresy. Irenaeus, the bishop of Lyons, who died around the year 202, wrote a lengthy treatise called *Against Heresies*, in which he denounced movements and individuals deemed outside the theological mainstream,

THE BISHOP

Our times are so different than the early church. We rarely spend much time defending the humanity of Jesus, instead stumbling to articulate his divinity in a persuasive way.

particularly the gnostics, and especially the group formed around an individual named Valentinus. According to Irenaeus, Valentinus taught that human beings were a combination of animal substance and spiritual substance, the former created by the Demiurge, a lesser god, and the latter formed by Achamoth, the transcendent, lofty deity. The "spiritual men" (gnostics) claimed to have "attained to the perfect knowledge of God, and been initiated into these mysteries by Achamoth."[4]

Clement of Alexandria, another second-century writer, reported that Valentinus even extended the implications of gnostic claims that Jesus only seemed (*dokein*) to be human, "exercising his divinity" by eating and drinking "in a peculiar manner, not evacuating his food." Thus, "so much power of continence was in him that in him food was not corrupted, since he himself had no corruptibility."[5] Apparently, Jesus's full divinity had biological consequences—he never pooped!

Gnosticism was no monolithic movement. Gnostics offered multiple options for explaining issues of creation, human nature, sinfulness, spirituality, and ultimately how the ways of God were made known to a spiritual minority of the human race. It represented one of the church's first great heresies, denounced by multitudes of Christian leaders for departing from or simply co-opting elements of Christian belief into unchristian ideologies. In reality, gnosticism reflected another response to Christianity, another reading of biblical and nonbiblical texts, and a way of explaining the mysteries surrounding the meaning of Jesus as God in the flesh.

## Explaining the God/Man: Orthodoxy and Heresy

Gnostics were only the first of the *flaming heretics* to appear on the Christian scene. Multiple ideas (and heresies) developed *inside* proto-orthodox Christianity regarding issues related to Jesus and the meaning of his divine/human status before and after he was "born of the Virgin Mary." The biblical texts were both encouraging and problematic. Jesus asserted, "I and the Father are one" (John 10:30); and "I am in the Father and the Father in me" (John 14:11). But he also declared, "My Father is greater than I" (John 14:28). John's Gospel begins with the affirmation, "In the beginning was the Word [*Logos*] and the Word was with God, and the Word was God" (John 1:1); but Paul also suggests that Jesus was "the image of the invisible God, the firstborn of every creature" (Colossians 1:15).

---

So the virgin conception of Jesus was used to protect his humanity? I totally hear that in the opposite direction these days.

THE ACOLYTE

---

The early church clearly had its work cut out for it in order to make the case for the uniqueness of Jesus in the world and the reasons why the death of a Nazarene rabbi on a Roman cross had salvific implications for the entire human race. They also had to explain the ways in which a monotheistic vision of God inherited from Judaism could make room either for three Gods—Father, Son, Spirit—or, as the hymn would later define it, "God in three persons, blessed Trinity." The debates and divisions over that simple affirmation shook the early church, creating aftershocks that have affected the church throughout history. Theories for explaining or at least responding to these issues were a drachma a dozen. Pay your money and take your choice.

## Logos Christology

Some said that Jesus was the incarnation of a spirit or emanation from God the Father, who had inspired and enlightened individuals since the Creation. Around the year 147, our old friend Justin Martyr wrote: "We have been taught that Christ is First-begotten of God and we have indicated . . . that He is the Word (*Logos*) of whom all humanity partakes. Those who lived by reason are Christians, even though they have been considered atheists: such as . . . Socrates, Heraclitus, and others . . . and . . . Abraham, Elijah, and . . . many others whose deeds and names we now forbear to enumerate, for we think it would be too long [a list]."[6]

In defending Christianity, Justin envisioned Christians before Christ, "enlightened pagans" whose lives and insights bore limited but faithful influence of the word of

God before it became flesh in Jesus. Yet he also suggested that "they who lived before Christ and did not live by reason were useless persons, enemies of Christ, and murderers of those who did not live by reason. But those who have lived reasonably, and still do, are Christians, and are fearless and untroubled."[7] Logos Christology suggested that the "light that enlightened everyone" had come into the world fully in Jesus, but the source of revelation had made itself known across the centuries.

---

JC has a Logos Christology! (John Cobb that is.)

---

## Monarchians: The Oneness of God

Other Christians rejected this idea in order to protect the "oneness" of God by finding ways to fit three into one. So-called Modalistic Monarchians believed that the Father, Son, and Spirit were simply "modes," or temporary expressions of the one God. The doctrine took shape in Rome by 190, promoted by a recent arrival named Noetus, who was dismissed from his congregation in Asia Minor for views they determined to be heretical. In Rome, he was joined by another presbyter named Sabellius, who became such a major proponent of modalism that the doctrine was later referred to as Sabellianism, a term used throughout Christian history to designate heresy of one sort or the other.[8] One of the best-known dogmas of the Modalistic Monarchians was *Patripassianism*, the belief that the Father was present not simply with, but in Christ on the cross, experiencing his suffering for the sins of the world. Noetus noted: "If therefore I acknowledge Christ to Be God, He is the Father Himself, if He is indeed God."[9] Thus all of God was both expressed and present in the *mode* that was Jesus, for indeed, Paul had written, "God was *in* Christ, reconciling the world to God's own self."

---

THE BISHOP

I think there may be more monotheist Christians than Trinitarian ones these days. I love the Trinity, but wonder if you can grasp it and love it without first learning the story of the doctrine itself.

---

Hippolytus, a Roman bishop and theologian, labeled Noetus a person "greatly puffed up and inflated with pride. . . . [Noetus] alleged that Christ was the Father Himself, and that the Father Himself was born, and suffered and died." This idea was born of "pride of heart," and "inflation by a strange spirit" insinuating itself into him.[10]

The proto-orthodox leaders of the second- and third-century church thought that the Monarchian views obliterated the uniqueness of Christ's divine presence in the world, and his continued presence through the Holy Spirit, a blow to the doctrine of the Trinity that was forming and being clarified. Writers like Hilary of Poitiers, Tertullian, and Hippolytus asserted that the Son was an eternal and unique personality of the Godhead, not a mere temporary form.[11]

"Dynamic Monarchians" were those who believed that Jesus was a "mere man" (*philos anthropos*) on whom God bestowed the power (*dynamis*). This was understood as a form of adoptionism, interpreted through texts such as Paul's comment that "God has made him [Jesus] both Lord and Christ." Again, the proto-orthodox leaders condemned this view as undercutting the uniqueness of the incarnation and the true divinity of Jesus.[12]

Devotees of both doctrinal outlooks were ultimately labeled heretics by the theological majority, yet their views were not lost to later Christians. Indeed, the label "Sabellian" was often thrown at groups and individuals who placed emphasis on the centrality of Jesus as containing the fullness of God. For example, Michael Servetus, the sixteenth-century Anabaptist and scientist, burned at the stake in Geneva, Switzerland, with the approval of John Calvin, was considered a Sabellian because he questioned the doctrine of the Trinity.

Within the more recent Pentecostal tradition, the "Jesus Only," or "Oneness" Pentecostals are often associated with Sabellian doctrines because of their belief that Jesus is the central expression of the one God, that baptism should be administered in the "name of Jesus only," and that with the incarnation all of God was present in Jesus (Patripassianism).

## Arius and Arianism: "There was when He was not"

Perhaps the most infamous "heresy" of the fourth-century church was perpetuated by Arius, a presbyter in the church of Alexandria, Egypt. Arius, who died in 336, believed that God (the Father) alone was present throughout eternity. Jesus, therefore, was a created being, formed by God in the beginning, as "the firstborn of all creation." He could be considered God but was clearly subordinate to the Father. Thus Arius contended of Jesus, "there was [a time] when He was not"; and "before he was begotten [created] He was not." Arius's critics, including his bishop, Alexander of Alexandria (I'm not kidding), were quick to challenge his views and declare them outside the orthodox norms, an attack on the very deity of Christ and the meaning of the Holy Trinity.

---

THE BISHOP

Poor Alexander. That is almost as bad as the second and third pope's name. Google it.

---

The Arian controversy divided the church down to the grassroots of the laity. It was said that in Constantinople, when you went to buy bread, the baker might ask if you believed "there was when he was not." Or if you wanted admission to the baths, you would be asked if you believed "before he was begotten, he was not."

Lest we suppose this is strictly a fourth-century phenomenon, it is worth acknowledging that in the early twenty-first century, when it was announced that the School of Divinity at Wake Forest University would follow the university policy and admit LGBT-oriented ministerial students to the Master of Divinity degree program, an event occurred that bore strange similarity to Arianism centuries before. When a staff member from the university ordered lunch for a group of divinity school faculty, her order was canceled when the cashier discovered the food's destination. No sandwiches would be served to faculty at a school that admitted gays and lesbians to study for the Christian ministry. Some things never change.

---

That is a sad story, but Wake Forest University couldn't be too surprised since their mascot is a Demon Deacon.

THE ELDER

---

## Creeds: Setting the Boundaries of Faith

"I believe"; that's what the word *credo* means. Creeds are statements of belief, basic summaries suggesting the rudiments of Christian faith, the bottom line of basic doctrines. In the church's history, creeds serve multiple purposes. First, creeds really began as baptismal statements, confessions of faith made at the high moment of entry into Christ and his church. Second, creeds are highly pragmatic. They delineate the minimal beliefs necessary for claiming to be Christian. Third, creeds are liturgical devices for affirming faith within the community of faith. In many Christian traditions, creeds are an integral part of communal worship—they can be sung as well as read. Fourth, creeds can become checklists for evaluating those considered heretical. They are tools for confessing faith and for separating true faith from false. Finally, and particularly with the Protestant Reformation, some groups and individuals eschewed what they often called "man-made creeds" altogether, insisting that "we have no creed but the Bible," or "we have no creed but Christ," and rejecting what many felt were nonbiblical structures of belief imposed by religious establishments implicit and explicit.

## The Council of Nicaea: "Of the same substance"

The Council of Nicaea illustrates all of those dynamics. When the Arian controversy threatened the stability of the Roman Empire, Emperor Constantine, hoping that the church would provide much-needed unity, intervened, calling what became the first of two millennia of ecumenical councils, in this case involving some 300 representatives of major dioceses, primarily from the Eastern Church. The vast majority were anti-Arian, so much so that when the vote came on the Creed of Nicaea, only two "no" votes were counted. The creed made use of a nonbiblical word, *homoousios*, to describe the relationship between God the Father and God the Son, affirming that they were of the same *substance* in their very beings. Arius, of course, insisted that they were *heterousios*, of different substance. Eusebius of Caesarea, the church's first historian, unsuccessfully urged the council to avoid nonbiblical language altogether.

The Creed of Nicaea contains both affirmation and condemnation. The first half offered an affirmation of what the majority of "proto-orthodox" theologians believed were the non-negotiable dogmas of apostolic Christianity. "We believe in one God the Father all powerful, maker of all things both seen and unseen. And in one Lord Jesus Christ, the Son of God, the only-begotten, begotten from the Father, that is, from the substance (*ousias*) of the Father, God from God, light from light, true God from true God, begotten not made, of the same substance (*homoousion*) with the Father, through whom all things came to be, both those in heaven and those in earth; for us humans and for our salvation he came down and became incarnate, became human, suffered and rose up on the third day, went up into the heavens, is coming to judge the living and the dead. And in the Holy Spirit."

---

**THE DEACON**

It might not be history, but the story of St. Nicholas slapping Arius with his sandal for denying Christ's full divinity and being thrown in prison during the council proceedings, only to have Arius visited by Mother Mary, is super sweet. Perfect for a Christmas children's sermon.

---

As noted in the introduction to this chapter, the second half of the creed condemns all who affirmed Arianism: "These the Catholic and apostolic Church anathematizes." The creed gives and the creed takes away. Arius and all who followed him were *flaming heretics*!

## The Irony of Anathema

Arianism was condemned. Proto-orthodoxy was victorious. Arians were excommunicated. All's right with the church.

But not so fast. Arians did not take anathema lying down. Before we know it, Arian leaders such as Eusebius, the bishop of Nicomedia (one of the two bishops voting against the Creed of Nicaea) gained great power in Constantine's court, even baptizing the emperor on his deathbed! So church and empire experienced years of Arian ups and down in terms of imperial power and privilege. Ultimately, Arians were exiled to the edges of the empire, so when the so-called "barbarian" tribes from Northern Europe—Vandals, Goths, Visigoths, et al.—crashed through those borders, many were first evangelized by the anathematized Arians.

Even so, come Lord Jesus! And that was not the end. Today's historical Unitarianism traces its origins to Arius's understanding of the nature of God and the person of Jesus.

## No Salvation outside the Church: The Roots of Excommunication

If the seeds of anathema and excommunication were sowed by Paul in Corinth, they were cultivated by later Christian writers such as Cyprian, the bishop of Carthage. Somewhere around the year 250, at the height of persecution against Christianity, Cyprian, who would himself be martyred in 258, wrote a treatise titled *On the Unity of the Catholic Church*, in which he declared: "No one who forsakes the Church of Christ can receive the rewards of Christ. He is a stranger; he is profane; he is an enemy. No one can have God for his Father, who does not have the Church for his mother."[13] This assertion provided the framework for the idea that there was no salvation outside the normative, proto-theological church grounded in the creeds and "rule of faith" (scripture, tradition, classic dogmas) and traceable to the apostles. It also became more enforceable when "Catholic [universal] Christianity" became the "normative" religion in the Roman Empire beginning with Constantine.

Excommunication would become an elaborate method of dealing with heretics, dissenters, and social deviants for generations. The concern was originally to encourage persons who had fallen away from orthodoxy or had crossed the church's moral boundaries to repent and be restored to the church's forgiving fellowship. Later on it became a religious/political method for dealing with recalcitrant monarchs, corrupt officials, or heretical sectarians. Catholics set the pattern, but many Protestant groups took up the cause, excommunicating, disciplining, shunning, or "unchurching" those whose beliefs or actions contradicted particular orthodoxies.

---

I wonder how many members of the early church were informed and participating in all the theological politics?

THE ACOLYTE

---

## Rending the "Seamless Robe of Christ": The Road to the Great Schism

Such unity couldn't last forever. Multiple controversies divided the church theologically and geographically over the nature of the human-and-divine in Jesus, the ongoing question of forgiveness of post-baptismal sin, and the role of particular bishops and patriarchs. The lattermost struggles were particularly pronounced after Constantine divided the empire into East and West, with capitols in Rome and Constantinople. The Bishop of Rome (the pope) and the Patriarch of Constantinople, along with assorted Roman Emperors, vied for power and influence in various controversies. Divisions theological, liturgical, demographic, and personal came and went until 1054 when Michael Cerularius, the Patriarch of Constantinople, took actions that seemed to undermine respect for the pope in Rome and the presence of Western Christians in Constantinople. Among other things, Cerularius charged that Christians of the Western rites were theologically questionable because they had added a phrase to the Nicene Creed, stating that the Holy Spirit "proceeds from the Father, *and the Son*," what many Eastern Christians felt was a heretical violation of the infallible action of the Council of Nicaea.

THE ACOLYTE

Hey, professor, is there going to be a test on all these names?

Finally, Pope Leo IX sent his representatives with a document to Patriarch Cerularius, delivered on July 16,

1054. It read: "Let them be anathema maranatha; with Simoniacs, Valerians, Arians, Donatists, Nicholaitans, Pneumatomachi, Manichees, Nazarenes, and with all other heretics, yea with the devil and his angels. Amen and Amen."

The list of other *flaming heretics* was considerable and poignant. The division was deep and continues to this day between Roman Catholic and Eastern Orthodox Christians. Dialogue between the two churches has improved somewhat. But the historical anathema remains.

---

THE ELDER

Just imagine how this would have gone down if there was Twitter and twenty-four-hour partisan news. The *Filioque* News Network!

---

## Martin Luther: "A Wild Boar Is Loose"

As word of Martin Luther's challenge to papal authority and the selling of indulgences broke across the church in 1517, the Roman Pontiff, Leo X, dismissed it as simply the ravings of a Saxon monk drinking too much German beer. But as events accelerated, and under advice from prominent bishops and theologians, the pope issued a *bull* threatening excommunication if Luther did not recant. In January 1521, Pope Leo X placed a papal ban on Luther in a document known as *Exsurge Domine*, which began, "Arise, O Lord, and judge they cause. A wild boar has invaded thy vineyard."[14] It rejected some forty-four of Luther's claims against orthodox doctrine and practice, urged him to forsake his "pernicious errors," and ordered him to stop preaching his views.[15] Luther and his students burned the document in the streets of Wittenberg.

In response to that action, Leo X issued a bull that became known as *Decet Romanum*, excommunicating Martin Luther and any who protected him from the Roman Church. It declared: "Our decrees which follow are passed against Martin and others who follow him in the obstinacy of his depraved and damnable purpose, as also against those who defend and protect him in the obstinacy of his depraved and damnable purpose. . . . On all these we decree the sentences of excommunication, of anathema, of our perpetual condemnation and interdict; of privation of dignities, honours and property on them and their descendants. . . ."[16] The Reformation began with anathemas.

## Reformation Protestantism: Heretics against Heretics

One of the real ironies of the Protestant Reformation is that many of its heretics, anathematized by Rome, became heresy hunters themselves, often with violent results. Ulrich Zwingli, the reformer of Zurich, was killed in 1531 during a battle against the Swiss Catholic militias, and he was condemned as a heretic by the pope. But before his death, he participated in the execution of Felix Mantz, an early leader among the Swiss Brethren, who was condemned to death by the Zurich city council for refusing to have his child baptized. By edict of the city council, Mantz was drowned in the Lammat River on January 5, 1527, for his perceived heretical views on believer's baptism. He was the first Protestant to die at the hands of Protestants.

We have already noted John Calvin's approval of the burning of Michael Servetus, condemned for his heretical views on the nature of the Trinity. In England, the prominent humanist writer and churchman, Sir Thomas More, instigated the torture and death of numerous persons condemned as heretics for their Protestant views. The *Catholic Encyclopedia* notes that as Lord Chancellor during the reign of Henry VIII, More "had no hesitation" in enforcing anti-heresy laws against Protestants, before England itself went Protestant. The *Encyclopedia* article observes that More "never proceeded to extremities [torture and death] until he made every effort to get those brought before him to recant. How successful he was in this is clear from the fact that only four persons suffered the supreme penalty for heresy during his whole term of office."[17] Ironically (again), when Henry VIII broke with Rome over "the King's Great Matter" of divorce and remarriage, Thomas More refused to acquiesce to the Act of Supremacy recognizing Henry as "Supreme Head of the Church on earth in England." Condemned for treason because of his support for papal authority, More was beheaded in 1535. During the Reformation era, the definition of heresy could turn on a dime.

---

I don't know about you, but I keep thinking of the TV shows *The Tudors* and *The Borgias* throughout the chapter. When will HBO release *When the Son Was Not . . . ?*

THE DEACON

---

## Galileo: When Heresy and Modernity Collide

The list of heresies and heretics seems endless in Christian history, intensifying and moderating with the rise of the modern era, complicated with the development of new knowledge and discoveries in science, sociology, psychology, biblical studies, and other areas of modern thought. Moderation, if we may call it that, meant that with the changes in various nations and cultures there was at least an emerging trend toward greater religious toleration if not a complete religious freedom. (This was all hard won, and not uniform, even into the twenty-first century.) This meant heresy trials, denunciations, excommunications, and exilings might continue, but fewer people got burned at the stake. It also meant that heretics in one era became heroes later on as their views or discoveries gained scientific or philosophical acceptance. Galileo's story anticipated the future.

In Scene One of Bertolt Brecht's play, *Galileo*, a boy named Andrea enters the scientist's room carrying "a big astronomical model" showing earth at the center of the cosmos, an idea attributed to the ancient philosopher Ptolemy. Earth is thus surrounded by eight spheres that chart the sun and the planets as they revolve around the "fixed globe in the middle." Galileo explains: "That's the earth. For two thousand years man has chosen to believe that the sun and all the host of stars revolve around him." Andrea responds: "I can see with my own eyes that the sun comes up one place in the morning and goes down in a different place in the evening. It doesn't stand still—I can see it move. To which Galileo responds: "You see nothing, all you do is gawk. Gawking is not seeing."[18]

Now *that* is a line every minister should save for special occasions.

**THE DEACON**

Born in Pisa, Italy, Galileo Galilei (1564–1642) never married, but fathered three children. His two daughters became nuns, a protective option for females born of unmarried parents. Galileo's correspondence with his daughter Virginia (Sister Maria Celeste) provides perhaps the most informative picture of his personal and public life.[19]

The greatest astronomer of his time, Galileo made extensive use of the newly invented telescope, discovering the existence of sunspots, moonscapes (mountains and valleys, not smooth as previously thought), and the role of the tides in charting earth's axis (he was right about tides, though wrong on some details). These findings led to increased support for the heliocentric theory set forth in Copernicus's work, *On the Revolutions of the Heavenly Spheres*, in 1543. By 1616, Galileo was defending the Copernican assertion that the earth revolved around the sun, not vice versa. That same year the Inquisition condemned the theory as "foolish and absurd in philosophy, and formally heretical since it explicitly contradicts . . . the sense of Holy Scripture, according to the literal meaning of the words and according to the common interpretation and understanding of the Holy Fathers."[20]

Catholic church leaders viewed Galileo's assertions as contradicting biblical texts including the day the sun "stood still" (Joshua 10:13); and in 1 Chronicles 16:30, "the world cannot be moved." Cardinal Robert Bellarmine ordered Galileo "to abandon completely" the view "that the sun stands still at the center of the world and the earth moves . . . or defend it in any way whatever, either orally or in writing." Galileo acquiesced. Brecht has an "Old Cardinal" declare "I won't have it! I won't be a nobody on an inconsequential star briefly twirling hither and thither. . . . The earth is the center of all things, and I am the center of the earth, and the eye of the Creator is upon me."[21]

Galileo then slipped under the ecclesiastical radar until 1632 when he published *Dialogue on the Great World Systems, Ptolemaic and Copernican*, affirming heliocentricism. The new pope, Urban VIII, a humanist-oriented advocate of scientific pursuits, was taken by surprise, and distressed that Galileo neglected to include a disclaimer that God can create in multiple ways, all beyond human perception. Called to Rome, Galileo confronted the Inquisitors, who warned that failure to recant could have dire consequences. Brecht's Galileo comments: "I cannot afford to be smoked on a wood fire like a ham."[22]

---

**THE ELDER**

Avoiding the smoked pork treatment is very important to me. Luckily there are too many vegans at my church to even serve actual pork. Hummus for everyone.

---

Thus he confessed in 1633,

> After having been admonished by this Holy Office entirely to abandon the false opinions that the Sun is the center of the world and immovable, and that the Earth is not the center of the same and that it moves, and that I must not . . . defend, nor teach in any manner whatever, either orally or in writing, the said false doctrine, and after it has been notified to me that the said doctrine was contrary to Holy Writ . . . I abjure with a sincere heart and unfeigned faith, I curse and detest the said errors and heresies, and generally all and every error and sect contrary to the Holy Catholic Church.[23]

House arrest followed.

From a historical perspective (at least this historian's perspective) much of the ecclesiastical response to heresy and/or heretics has done more to discredit Christianity than promote it. In fact, years after the heretical fact, the church has wound up apologizing for its treatment of those thought to stray from the folds of orthodoxy. Religious faith is intense, no doubt about it, but heresy hunting often carries the church far afield from the principles it claims to hold most dear.

We all read the past through spectacles of the present, gawking our way to truth through faulty dogmas, theorems, proof-texts, and politics. Generations later, we finally *see*, recanting our recantations, and repenting of our forebears' torture-laden Inquisitions. Brecht's *Galileo* concludes:

*May you now guard science's light, Kindle it and use it right,*
*Lest it be a flame to fall, Downward to consume us all.*[24]

See?[25]

4

# Mother of God or the Devil's Gateway? Women and the Church

St. Jerome, the fourth-century biblical scholar, hermit, and misogynist, wrote: "As long as woman is for birth and children, she is different from man as body is from soul. But when she wishes to serve Christ more than the world, then she will cease to be a woman and will be called man" (*Comm. In Epis ad Eph.* III. 5).

---

THE ACOLYTE

Excuse me while I clean up my vomit. This is why celibate hermits should not talk about gender, sex, or reproduction. Who made him a saint, anyway?

---

Sojourner Truth, the nineteenth-century former slave, abolitionist, preacher, and human rights advocate, was once confronted by a man who responded to her impassioned opposition to chattel slavery by saying: "Old woman, do you think your talk about slavery does any good? Do you suppose people care what you say? Why, I don't care any more for your talk than I do for the bite of a flea."

"Perhaps not," Sojourner Truth replied, "but Lord willing, I'll keep you scratching."[1]

Jerome's statement captures something of the official attitude of many (dare we say most) of the church's male theologians (we call them the "Fathers") during the post-apostolic period and beyond. Sojourner Truth's exchange with another male, almost 2,000 years later, illustrates something of the response of women in Christian history, both to the roles that have been forced upon them and roles they have forged for themselves. Yet across the centuries, women have kept the church "scratching" with prophetic insight and action, both welcomed and unwelcomed, by the church's male leaders, Catholic, Orthodox, or Protestant.

From the beginning, Christianity manifested both affirmation and hesitancy toward the presence of women in the church. The story of Jesus's birth opens when a woman named Mary is told she is to bear "the son of the most High" (Luke 1:30). Within a few hundred years, Mother Mary was revered as *theotokos*, God-bearer, a status so exalted that she was even referred to as "the new Eve," since her son was the "the new Adam." In 1854, Pope Pius IX declared that the ever-virgin Mary "in the first instance of her conception, by a singular privilege and grace granted by God, in view of the merits of Jesus Christ, the Savior of the human race, was preserved exempt from all stain of original sin."[2] Thus the Immaculate Conception of the Blessed Virgin Mary became dogma of the Roman Catholic Church. The *Documents of Vatican II* sums it up by asserting that "the Mother of God is a model of the Church in the matter of faith, charity, and perfect union with Christ." The document affirms, "She was the new Eve, who puts her absolute trust not in the ancient serpent but in God's messenger."[3]

Women were among Jesus's first followers by the Sea of Galilee, and he interacts with them all along the way, often challenging the conventions of first-century culture and religion. In John chapter 4, for example, Jesus's encounter with a Samaritan woman, the so-called "woman at the well," is a powerful example of his response to females literally in his path. In this story, Jesus violates all the social, ritual, theological, doctrinal, racial, religious, gender, demographic, ethical, and cosmological boundaries of his day, with a woman who, according to religion and social convention, did not in the slightest deserve to be chosen. Jesus breaks every rule: talking to her; asking to share her water—oblivious to the "separate but equal" rule regarding Jewish/Samaritan facilities; takes her theological commentary seriously; and compromises his already questionable reputation by dialoguing with a woman whose sexual escapades were so notorious that even strangers passing through had heard of them. And that's only one of Jesus's interaction with females outside the boundaries of custom and religious regulations.

THE BISHOP

I think the continued presence of the Gospels within the church kept the door cracked for women and we are just now starting to open the door to a church beyond patriarchy. The struggle continues.

Yet certain Christian regulations regarding women's presence, particularly but not exclusively as set forth by Paul—including, but not limited to: "I suffer not a woman to teach" and "wives be subject to your husbands"—worked their way into the life of the church. Such biblical passages defined certain "women's spheres" that set limits not only on their activities, but also their identity within the community of faith. The woman's sphere set boundaries for women, even as many women utilized those spheres to provide significant contributions to the church and develop significant power, often in ways never intended by the men who set the rules and the limits.

## Woman as Virgin (the Patristic Period and Beyond)

The Fathers of the church struggled with a doctrine of the "Fall" of Eve and Adam and in so doing shaped theology, doctrine, and much popular opinion for determining women's role in church and society.

These "Fathers" definitely struggled, but the number of women who struggled in their wake is much greater.

**THE ACOLYTE**

Many showed particular concern to interpret the words of Genesis 1:27, "in the image of God he created him; male and female he created them," in ways that distinguished male and female from the moment of creation. Augustine and others interpreted this to mean that the image of God (*imago Dei*) and maleness were integrally related. Femaleness, on the other hand, concerned only "the lower, corruptible, bodily nature." In fact, Augustine wrote that in the divine scheme of things, "woman was given to man, woman who was of small intelligence and who perhaps still lives more in accordance with the promptings of the inferior flesh than by human reason."[4] Thus Rosemary Radford Ruether suggests that as far as the church's "fathers" were concerned, Eve is Adam's "helpmeet" primarily for the purpose of procreation, an "indispensable" role for females. Otherwise, males would be more preferable as helpmeets on life's journey.[5]

Augustine wrote: "Then she is not the image of God, as regards the male alone, but he is the image of God as fully and completely as when the woman too is joined with him is one."[6] So Ruether concludes that the female body reflects less of the image of God than simply a physical condition very subordinate to the male. Women served as the constant reminder of the nature of the Fall and the reality of sin.[7] For Augustine, their relationship with the Divine image is more derivative than direct.

In many of these writers, women are of a lesser nature than man, and in that nature they have both the seeds of life and the seeds of sin. They are agents of reproduction, birthing offspring who reflect the image of God and bear the curse of original sin. The Fall occurred, Augustine believed, when the "male ruling principle agreed to 'go along'" with the female and fall into sin.[8] Thus Eve's sin is terrible because she, not the serpent, seduced him who held the full image of God.

---

**THE ELDER**

I remember when the first wave of feminism washed onto my church's shore. It was a thunderous crash into the seawall of patriarchy. Now I read this history and shiver with disgust, grateful to the erosion from each feminist wave.

---

Tertullian wrote of woman, "*You* are the Devil's gateway; *you* are the unsealer of that tree; *you* are the first forsaker of the divine law; *you* are the one who pursued him whom the devil was not brave enough to approach; *you* so lightly crushed the image of God, the man Adam."[9]

Woman could escape her evil nature by living in the Spirit, beyond the body. She could remain—indeed, become—a virgin, not simply in body but in spirit. Through virginity woman escaped the curse of Eve in childbearing and male domination. She could then nurture "manly" virtues over slavery to the flesh.[10]

---

Didn't Tertullian turn into a Montanist with female prophets? He really should have posted a retraction.

THE ACOLYTE

---

Virginity in males restored the image of God, and virginity in females made women more male, i.e., restoring image of God. Thus, some early Christian writers thought that in the resurrection there would be only male bodies—the resurrection body was a male body. Jerome and Augustine deny this in favor of a male/female androgynous union without sexuality.[11]

In many respects several of the church fathers view women as dangerous sexual objects, representing lust, sin, and the flesh. As wives they are to be subject to their husbands, with a primary role in procreation and the continuation of the race. Yet they also value those women who choose virginity, relinquish childbearing, and thus pursue greater spirituality and personhood.

Augustine agreed that marriage represented God's plan for regulating lust and propagating the race. He wrote, "The natural good of marriage is thus sexual intercourse between male and female for the sake of procreation." Yet even marital sex was inappropriate when it was provoked by lust or desire rather than simply for reproduction.[12] Sex, therefore, is best when unfeeling and for procreation only. It is a bodily and therefore sinful power that has a will of its own and leads to irrational sensual pleasure.[13]

---

THE DEACON

I am guessing Augustine was not the best at premarital counseling.

---

For Augustine, the sex act, even in marriage, did not restore a prevenient (unfallen) state since it inevitably produces the "filthy acts" of carnal pleasure. But the couple is forgiven if this is involuntary and dispensable. Nonetheless, Augustine believes, "Whatever offspring is born is liable to original sin unless it is reborn in him whom the Virgin conceived without this lust."[14] Baptism of newborns is absolutely necessary to cure the curse of original sin. Mary, the "new Eve," was a participant in the restoration or "recapitulation" of the human race to its pre-fallen state.

To enjoy sex apart from procreation is especially sinful though it is permitted through scripture admonition: "better to marry than to burn" (1 Corinthians 7:9). If the couple intends only sexual pleasure, not procreation, then the act is equivalent to fornication. Children are a good end of procreation though tainted by these "debased means," thus, without a "spiritual birth" (baptism) they are damned.[15]

Augustine also addresses homosexuality, citing Romans 1:27 which references "abandoning the natural use" of sex in both men and women. He concludes that "to use a part of the body that was not meant for procreation is against nature and disgraceful, even if a man is having sexual relations with his wife." For married couples to engage in such behavior (one supposes anal sex) is exceptionally "impure and defiled" since it is sex with no possibility of procreation.[16]

## Ever-Virgin: The Pursuit of Celibacy

Very early in Christian history virginity and celibacy became important options for persons choosing to live in the Spirit, anticipating the imminent return of Christ (thus procreation was less an issue), and as a means of winning the battle over the flesh. Paul clearly recommended celibacy as a valuable lifestyle that freed the individual for greater activism in behalf of the gospel, using himself as the model (1 Corinthians 7:28–36). Others saw it as a form of martyrdom for those seeking to live holy lives, conquering lust and the "lower nature."

Jerome, best known for his translation of the Bible into Latin (*Vulgate*), was a great advocate of virginity, but acknowledged its difficulties, writing, "Do not fear that all will become virgins: virginity is a difficult business and is rare just because it is hard." He also noted that in the late fourth century when he was writing, many persons attempted to undertake virginity, but "to stick with it is for the few—whence also the reward for those who have persevered is great."[17] Jerome admits that he does not disparage marriage, but insists that "chastity was always to be preferred to the marital relationship."[18]

Jerome, who in his youth was not celibate, writes with great disgust for intercourse and pregnancy. How, he says, could one such experience, terrible as it is, lead to another? In fact, he sees childbirth and procreation as palatable primarily if children are raised as virgins; he even praising weddings and marriages "because they produce virgins for me."[19]

---

Regardless of the context, I suggest no minister include the phrase "because they produce virgins for me" during a wedding celebration.

---

Jerome gathered a group of pious women whom he instructed in Christian living and virginity, with particular advice for mothers who dedicated their daughters to a life of virginity. He suggested that youthful virgins not bathe with eunuchs or pregnant women, and that the child should essentially be kept secluded to avoid corruption by society. She should best have no contact with men, even eunuchs; and no contact with pregnant women or married women. Even bathing was a problem. Jerome wrote of his disapproval of all bathing "for a virgin of full age," since she would "feel overcome" by her own nakedness.

Resistance to bathing was also helpful since through such "deliberate squalor she makes haste to spoil her natural good looks." He insisted that younger virgins should go out in public only when accompanied by their mothers, adding, "Let no young man greet her with smiles, no dandy with curled hair pay compliments to her."[20]

Female virgins should watch their diets, and receive proper instructions in appropriate methods of fasting, especially how to avoid fleshly foods that enflame one's desires (tacos? pizza?).

---

And I thought
*I Kissed Dating Goodbye*
was rough!

THE DEACON

---

Virginity, Jerome believed, enhanced female intellect, as evident in their ability to grasp Greek, Hebrew, and biblical exegesis more readily. However, they were not to tout those skills, lest they betray the modesty of the female role.[21]

The idea of Christian virginity reflects a paradox in the patristic church. In one sense, women were viewed as subordinate, inferior in creation, agents of sin, and spiritually backward. Their only hope was to become more male by escaping the "bonds of womanhood"—sex, childbirth, and marriage. Yet as virgins, they were often granted unique authority in the church. Virgins or widows were more readily chosen deaconesses, officers who offered pastoral care for women matters in the early church. Deaconesses were present at interviews between pastors and women. They helped maintain order in the women's section of the church. (Males and females sat in separate areas at worship.) They also prepared women for baptism. With the decline of adult baptism by the fifth century came the decline of the office of deaconess.

Virginity was a factor in the development of female monastic life. In these monastic communities, women achieved significant ecclesiastical leadership, produced an impressive collection of spiritual literature, and developed varying degrees of influence on church affairs. Virginity freed women from the demands of childbirth and allowed time to cultivate other gifts and callings—within the boundaries of ecclesiastical order.

Nowhere is virginity more exalted than in the evolution of devotion to the Blessed Virgin Mary. She epitomized all the virtues of womanhood extolled by the early Fathers. Mary remains a model of virginal faithfulness, but she is also unique in her relationship to Christ and to his church.

## Woman as Mother

The church's emphasis on woman as mother seems almost too obvious to discuss. It is, however, a less uniform idea than might be supposed. For example, during the thirteenth century, the theology of Thomas Aquinas informed the church's view of women in the married, mothering role. Marriage, though a sacrament, is the least favorable of Thomas's three particular roles for women. Virginity in women religious (nuns) is primary, widowhood being the second-most preferable option. (So for Thomas Aquinas, women whose husbands are dead are in a more appropriate state of life than women with live husbands!?)

Marriage, therefore, is a remedy for sin, particularly in women, who as child bearers, have the stronger sex drive and the least intellectual capacity to cope with it.[22]

Aquinas suggested that Eve's lack of intellect distinguished the *imago Dei* in her from the more superior male intellect and made her more easily seduced by the serpent.

---

What part of Adam being quiet and taking the fruit from Eve like a good boy makes him more intelligent?

THE ACOLYTE

---

Maleness was more active, powerful, and determinative than femaleness, which is more passive receptacle. So the male is the determinative force in sexual intercourse, procreation, and family. The father, Aquinas believes, is to be the nurturing, intellectual, educating force in the family.[23] (Let us note Aquinas's belief that Christ purposely took on male sexual identity because of its strength and intellect, its active, defending, redeeming qualities. That role is incompatible with the subordinate role of women. The priesthood, therefore, is an extension of Christ's work and thus maleness and priesthood are inseparable.)

The woman as mother in Thomistic thought is bound to childbirth. Yet to inhibit conception (birth control) is sinful, not because it upsets woman's role, but because it interferes with the natural and divinely ordained function of male sperm. In the resurrection, women will achieve that essential male quality—intellect—since they will be delivered from the curse of childbirth. Aquinas is among those medieval thinkers who, as good Aristotelians, divide flesh and spirit. Sex therefore, because it is associated with the flesh, cannot represent the highest ideal of love, which is primarily spiritual.[24]

Catholic theologian Elizabeth Johnson observes that Thomas Aquinas accepted "without question the subordination of women as the God-given order of the world."[25] She cites his now amazing comment that "the active power" of the male seed produced "something like itself perfect in masculinity," while procreation of females "is the result either of the debility of the active power, of some unsuitability of the material, or of some change effected by external influences."[26]

The Reformation brought new insight to the role of Christian mother. Luther and the Reformers essentially maintained a sense of subordination toward women, but also insisted that motherhood was as valid a Christian "vocation" as virginity or the cloister. Women could assert their spiritual role as wives and mothers as proudly as the nun or the virgin. This raised the status of marriage and family to a new religious plateau. At the same time, it placed women in an environment that kept them from exercising the ecclesiastical influence they had known in the monastery in an environment independent of men. It also created the idea of the "Protestant Mother" whose indirect influence on her children, particularly her sons, was the hallmark of the Christian home, fact and fiction.

But perhaps the Great Protestant Mother was Susanna Annesley Wesley, the matriarch of Methodism. Susanna

When I was young we watched VHS tapes of *Little House on the Prairie* in the church "Future Mothers of Virtue" program.

THE BISHOP

(1669–1742) gave birth to nineteen children, among them John and Charles. She taught each child the Lord's Prayer by the time each learned to talk, and began teaching them to read at age five. The children were home-schooled for six hours a day, and she spent time daily in private conversation with each child as to the state of his or her soul. She even composed a systematic theology text for her daughters.[27]

Susanna Wesley's correspondence with her son John while he was a student at Oxford reveals that nothing changes. A letter dated August 19, 1724, begins, "Dear Jacky: I am somewhat uneasy, because I've not heard from you so long. . . . Therefore let me hear from you oftener, and inform me . . . whether you . . . have any reasonable hopes of being out of debt."[28] I rest my case.

Many Methodist scholars suggest that her ordered home life provided the framework for her sons' methodical religious organization. Thus the Protestant woman was to effect religious life by virtue of her role as mother and nurturer and by the depth of her own piety passed on to her children—a worthy, enduring model.

Three important issues inform our understanding of Christian motherhood. First, it remains a valid and significant role, a fact often undermined in reaction to

THE DEACON

At least she didn't text him saying, "I am praying with deep concern for your regrettable religious doubts and credit score when you can't pay for your degree in heretical religion. Your father and I can't in good conscience support your schooling when it is clearly undermining your eternal security." (Don't worry, my mother isn't reading this book.)

some of its more mythological elements. Motherhood is being demythologized in our day but must also be remythologized as to its healthy place in society, church, and home. Second, it reflects a significant reality—that most of Christian history was pre-contraceptive history. Marriage meant babies—lots of babies—some lived, many died. Throughout most of the world's history women married young and had babies every nine to twelve months. High mortality rates for mothers and infants meant that by age thirty women had perhaps ten to twelve pregnancies, devoting time to childrearing, health, and home. This biological reality had theological implications.

For example, high infant mortality led many to question or modify the harsh statement in the Westminster Confession of Faith which read that only "*elect infants*, dying in infancy, shall be saved," a dogma that suggested the damnation of non-elect infants. The idea that mothers would lose their babies in this world and in the next was simply too great a burden to bear. Arminian Protestants insisted that infants were under grace until they were able to decide for salvation for themselves. The General (Arminian) Baptist "Standard Confession of Faith" of 1660 asserts "that all Children dying in infancy, having not actually transgressed against the Law of God in their own persons, are only subject to the first death, which comes upon them by the sin of the first Adam." Because of that, they would die, but not experience the "second death," eternal punishment, since "of such [children] are the kingdom of Heaven."[29]

---

**THE BISHOP**

These tragic concerns show up today for hospital chaplains. Infant baptism for a dying child is a test case for putting your tradition's theology over compassionate support of grieving parents.

---

Likewise, Mother Ann Lee, the Shaker founder, had multiple miscarriages before she received a revelation that sexual intercourse was the cause of Adam and Eve's fall, and began to preach celibacy as essential for a kingdom life. One early Shaker testimony noted that "by the immediate revelation of God," Mother Ann "bore an open testimony against the lustful gratifications of the flesh, as the source and foundation of human corruption." These insights made her "the first spiritual Mother in Christ, and the second heir of the *Covenant of Life*." Hence the second appearing of the Christ.[30] Shaker and other utopian communities became havens for abused women and children, as well as women seeking to escape the cycle of pregnancy. As a source of revelation and nurture, Mother Ann Lee became the spiritual nurturer during her life and even after her death when she was herself a source of new revelation and spiritualist appearances to members of the United Society of Believers in Christ's Second Appearing.

Third, recent transitions related to sociological, demographic, and familial structures suggest a more expansive approach to "motherhood," evident in "single-parent families" where women are more often the primary parent; "blended families" that bring together varying generations, divorced and remarried parents, and adopted or foster children. Likewise, "surrogate mothers," artificial insemination, and same-sex marriages bring men and women into varying types of "mothering" roles in family life. Redefinitions of motherhood will no doubt continue in the twenty-first century and beyond.

## Women as Spiritual Guides: The Inner Light

A third category for understanding the role of women in church history is that of spiritual guides. In this role women assume certain callings, vocations, and missions by virtue of having been apprehended by the Holy Spirit. Such a calling was often thought to transcend sexual distinction or ecclesiastical regulations. In this view the randomness and mystery of the Spirit knows neither male nor female. It was an elusive calling of the inner person, born of response to the overpowering Spirit, often a calling unsought and unwanted. Catholic mystic tradition provided a context whereby women transcended their traditional roles and made broad, lasting contributions to the entire church. A variety of Protestant women also demonstrated a depth of spirituality that made them spiritual mentors to women and men, often challenging traditional roles assigned, indeed foisted upon them in Protestant churches. Catholic women found ways to cultivate their gifts inside and alongside ecclesiastical regulations as these three illustrations indicate.

**Julian of Norwich (1342–1416/23)** Lady Julian was an English hermit who occupied a cell next to a church in Norwich. She is the first individual to write in the English language who is known for certain to have been female. Her *Revelations of Divine Love* offers sixteen visions with commentary, detailing spiritual experiences she had while ill in the year 1373. She discusses the Motherhood of God as evidenced in Jesus, noting that he is "our mother, our brother, our saviour. . . . And so Jesus is our true mother by nature, at our first creation, and he is our true mother in grace by taking on our created nature. . . . But Jesus is our true mother, feeding us not with milk, but with himself, opening his side for us and claiming all our love."[31] The mystical experience involves all-encompassing love. The *Revelations of Divine Love* remains an important resource for men and women alike.

**The Beguines (1207)** The Beguines were an order of laywomen who built communities, primarily in the Low Countries of Europe, establishing their first community in

1207. The women came together to care for one another, to give themselves to the nurture of the spiritual life, and to care for persons on the margins of medieval society. They took no vows, lived a celibate life, but were free to leave (and marry) if they wished. Beguine communities offered a third way for medieval women for whom the only choices were the cloister or marriage. They cultivated a spiritual life of prayer, contemplation, and mystical experience. Their spiritual/mystical speculation also led to their condemnation or at least suspicion by the Inquisition and condemnation by various church councils. Many church leaders accused them of heresy, yet their communities grew considerably, some with several thousand members, composed of persons of high and low social estate. The Beguines offered safe space to abused and homeless females, and provided spiritual guidance to persons who sought their counsel.

Perhaps the two best-known writers associated with the Beguines were Hadewijch of Antwerp and Mechthild of Magdeburg, both of whom lived in the thirteenth century. Hadewijch's letters and poetry form a body of spiritual literature; while Mechthild's visions and revelations were recorded in a work titled *The Flowing Light of the Godhead.* These works continue to provide spiritual guidance to twenty-first-century seekers.[32]

---

**THE ACOLYTE**

I think I just found some new heroes!

---

**Sor Juana de la Cruz (1651–1695)** Sor Juana de la Cruz, widely known in Mexico and South America, but little known in the U.S., was a nun, a scientist, a writer-poet, and a bridge between Old/New World cultures and religions. Born (out of wedlock) in 1651 in New Spain (Mexico) to a *Criolla* mother (American-born Spaniard) and Spanish military officer, she had a privileged education and entered the monastic life in 1677. She confessed that monastic life was in many respects "repugnant" to her nature, "but given the antipathy I felt for marriage, I deemed convent life the least unsuitable and the most honorable I could elect if I were to insure my salvation."[33] Ilan Stavans suggests that through her writing, primarily her poetry, Sor Juana "challenged the ecclesiastical status quo, but with a subtlety that confused her contemporaries; she fought for women's rights not with weapons but with poetry."[34] Some of Sor Juana's work was aimed at the evangelization of native peoples in the New World; it was also intended to demonstrate to the Spanish audience the dignity and complexity of Native Americans through the stories of their history and customs. In fact, it is perhaps the Spanish audience that will be evangelized.[35]

In a famous work known as the *Loa*, a play with characters representing America and Christian Religion, America declares, "For though my person come to harm, and though I weep for liberty, my liberty of will, will grow, and I shall still adore my Gods!"[36] The play urges America to find the true religion (Christianity) while also giving voice to America in reasserting its own religious identity. Unashamedly Christian, courageous in her poetic challenge to church authority, and giving voice to native peoples in her plays and poetry, Sor Juana de la Cruz must not be overlooked by those who seek a *guide* to the church's history.

In the United States, an African American preacher named Jarena Lee illustrates the challenge that females raised as they asserted their voices, their callings, and their response to the status quo.

**Jarena Lee (1783–1855?)** We know very little of Jarena Lee, a nineteenth-century African American evangelist and preacher, except for what she includes in the brief autobiography she left behind. Lee was converted at a service in which the preacher was Rev. Richard Allen, founder of the African Methodist Episcopal Church, and Baltimore pastor. She recalled, "That day was the first when my heart had believed, and my tongue had made confession unto salvation."[37]

Shortly after, she sought "entire sanctification of the soul to God." After a period of spiritual warfare with her soul, she received sanctification by the Holy Spirit.[38]

In 1811 Lee experienced "a voice which I thought I distinctly heard, and most certainly understood, which said to me, 'Go preach the Gospel!'"[39] She sought the counsel of Richard Allen who acknowledged her call, but suggested that it would be impossible to fulfill with the Methodists since their Book of Discipline made it impossible. Lee remarked, "For as unseemly as it may be now-a-days for a woman to preach, it should be remembered that nothing is impossible with God." After all, she concluded, since "the Saviour died for the woman as well as the man," why not women called to preach?[40] Her persistence led Richard Allen to support her work as "a traveling exhorter," but not a "licensed preacher."[41] The door to full ministerial recognition would remain closed.

Jarena Lee published two editions of her autobiography, the last in 1849. After that she was lost to history, with no discernible record of her death available. She summarized her ministry and her spirituality accordingly: "In my wanderings up and down among men, preaching according to my ability, I have frequently found families who told me that . . . while listening to hear what God would say by his poor coloured female instrument, have believed with trembling."[42] While she was "outside" the Methodist Book of Discipline, Jarena Lee remained true to her calling to provide spiritual guidance to those who sought it with and from her.

## The Long Walk Home: Breaking through the Church's "Woman's Sphere"

As this brief survey suggests, Jarena Lee was certainly not the only woman in Christian history to step outside an ecclesiastical "book of discipline" implicitly or explicitly, pushing against the boundaries of the "woman's sphere." As noted earlier, that sphere involved areas or attitudes of church life that were open to women, within certain confines of theology and praxis set for them. To vacate the sphere was to risk criticism, alienation from Christian community, accusations of heresy, or even personal threat. Yet, irony of ironies, women were and remain the largest active constituency for the church, from the apostolic era to the twenty-first century. Their presence shaped the church's spirituality, ministry, and, even when unacknowledged, the church's theology itself.

As we have seen, biological realities of pre-contraceptive childbirth were given theological interpretations connected to the fall of the race, original sin, and sexuality itself. Certain Pauline-related texts undergirded issues of women's mandated public "silence" in the church, or permitted women to teach women and children, but not men. The earliest woman's sphere set boundaries that emphasized females' vital roles in procreation, childbearing, and childrearing, yet paradoxically, an increasing emphasis on celibacy and the cloister provided a second option that permitted many women to expand their knowledge, their leadership skills, and their literary contributions. Likewise, women actively participated in the formation of new religious groups, from the second-century Montanist movement to the twenty-first-century Emerging Church movement.[43]

Yet, as historian Donald Mathews observes, a sense of female spirituality led segments of the church to create, for women, a religious "world which was theoretically acknowledged and valued by men but which they [men] could not penetrate."[44] Beyond that realm they could not go. Mathews describes nineteenth-century Southern evangelicalism in ways that sound strangely applicable to the larger church, noting: "It was almost as if men willingly conceded the moral superiority of women in order to prevent active female participation in worldly affairs."[45] Women were weak in matters of this world, strong in matters of the world to come. They had spiritual equality, perhaps even superiority to males, but functional inequality in the society and the church. Thus women could minister, but they could not be ministers, ordained that is.[46]

## "In Christ . . . neither male nor female": Christian History and the Paradox of Grace

Elizabeth Johnson asserts that feminist theologians like herself "love the vision of wholeness, equality, and freedom celebrated in an early baptismal hymn: in the oneness of Christ Jesus 'there is neither Jew nor Greek, neither slave nor free, neither male nor female'" (Galatians 3:28). But she also notes that this sense of gospel equality does not negate differences between males and females, or women themselves. Instead, she concludes, "it signifies an intrinsic valuation of women as human beings, created, sinful, redeemed, with all the dignity, rights, and responsibilities that accrue as a consequence." It is a "vision of a redeemed humanity."[47]

And therein may lie one of the church's great dilemmas, a radical gospel that crashes through all the spheres we create to set boundaries that divide, subordinate, or dehumanize other human beings. Sadly, in so many eras and cultures, the church of Jesus Christ has often overpromised and underdelivered such radical grace. Yet in era after era, in culture after culture, the liberating grace of the gospel broke through. Some twenty years after the ordination of Cindy Harp Johnson such liberation found me again at the ordination of Elizabeth Parker at the Ardmore Baptist Church, Winston-Salem, North Carolina. Nurtured to faith in that congregation, Elizabeth was in the first class of the School of Divinity, Wake Forest University, established in 1999. She graduated in 2002 and requested ordination as she moved into formal

Christian ministry. The service was packed with friends from church, community, and university. My spouse, Dr. Candyce Leonard and I attended the event, in the company of our daughter Stephanie, a person with special needs, then in her twenties. When it came time for the ancient ordination ritual almost the entire congregation came to the chancel to lay on hands and offer blessings. I shall never forget the sight of Stephanie Leonard placing her hands on Elizabeth Parker's head; a sign of ordination and liberation for all our special needs.

# 5

# Drawn from Immanuel's Veins: Salvation and Then Some

*"There is a fountain filled with blood, drawn from Immanuel's veins;*
*and sinners plunged beneath that flood, lose all their guilty stain."*[1]

William Cowper

My earliest memory of confronting (or being confronted by) the "plan of salvation" comes from the morning that Mr. Johnny Ramey decided to explain it to his Sunday school class of junior boys (eight-year-olds) at the First Baptist Church of Decatur, Texas. Mr. Ramey, a Baptist deacon who worked at the local Chevy dealership, left nothing to our imagination. We were sinners, he said, lost without hope of redemption in this world or the next. Christ's death on the cross and resurrection from the dead paid the price of our redemption. Without Jesus as personal Lord and Savior, we would wind up in hell, a terrible place of eternal punishment, wailing, and gnashing of teeth. Mr. Ramey was clear: if we put our faith in Christ and invited him into our pre-pubescent but discernibly sinful hearts, we would be saved. Needless to say, he got my attention, particularly his graphic description of that horrible nether world. (He meant us well, an early spiritual guide.)

---

THE DEACON

I remember this type of Sunday school lesson and even leading them before my faith got ruined by reading Bonhoeffer. It's hard for people to understand what it's like really believing everyone they know could potentially spend all eternity in conscious torment.

---

That Sunday school class generated a spiritual crisis in my eight-year-old universe. After several restless nights, I took up the matter with my family, who assured me of God's love, and packed me off to talk with our pastor. Soon afterwards, I walked the aisle of the First Baptist Church, confessed my faith in Jesus, and, on a cold January Texas night, received baptism (by immersion) in the name of Father, Son, and Holy Spirit. Thus my formal entry into Christ and his church began when Mr. Johnny Ramey scared hell out of me. I got saved.

## A Gospel of Salvation: Here Come the Gentiles

Whatever else it may involve, the Christian faith is about salvation, pure and simple. (Well, not always so simple!) The New Testament echoes that idea in memorable King James Bible phrases such as:

> "Except a man be born of water and of the Spirit he cannot enter the kingdom of God. (John 3:5)
>
> "Believe on the Lord Jesus Christ and thou shalt be saved." (Acts 16:31)
>
> "Repent and be baptized every one of you in the name of Jesus Christ for the remission of sins." (Acts 2:38)

Such salvation made one "a new creation" by which "everything has become new" (2 Corinthians 5:17).

The earliest Christians were clearly audacious (some thought downright zany) in asserting that the death of a Galilean Jew on a Roman cross had cosmic significance, with implications for every human being. At first, even the Christians had to be convinced. The Apostle Paul's contention that in Christ "there is no longer Jew or Greek, slave or free, male or female" (Galatians 3:26), had to be sold to a largely Jewish constituency. Many were not so sure that Gentiles could be grafted onto the covenant originally given only to Abraham and his seed. It took a while for them to let the Gentiles in. In fact, the expansion of salvation to the Gentiles remains one of the church's most radical revelations. God was in Christ, reconciling the world to God's own self (2 Corinthians 5:19).

At first, all this talk of salvation seemed relatively uncomplicated. "Believe on the Lord Jesus Christ and you will be saved," Paul told the Philippian jailer. But better hurry. Since Jesus's return was imminent, the word of salvation had to be proclaimed as broadly and passionately as possible. In the book of Acts, Simon Peter sums up the early plan of salvation offered to the entire human race. It is, he says, "the message God sent to the people of Israel, preaching peace by Jesus Christ." The story is simple, detailing "how God anointed Jesus of Nazareth with the Holy Spirit and with power; how he went about doing good and healing all who were oppressed by the devil, for God was with him. We are witnesses to all that he did both in Judea and in Jerusalem" (Acts 10:36–39).

As Peter tells it, Jesus Christ is the agent of global salvation, a radical redemption with immediate consequences. Indeed, Acts acknowledges the astonishment of "the circumcised believers" (Jewish Christians) at the realization that Gentiles were being included. And Peter asks an even more astounding question: "Can anyone withhold the water for baptizing these people who have received the Holy Spirit just as we have?" (Acts 10:44–47). Christianity got expansive quickly, at least where salvation was concerned. Extending the gospel to the Gentiles remains one of Christianity's most radical acts.

---

THE BISHOP

Radical indeed! It is hard to explain to my congregants that this meant through the Resurrected Christ and power of the Spirit, the church decided against the Torah and Jesus's actual disciples, to receive Gentile members based on confession without circumcision.

---

THE ELDER

God was still speaking after Jesus and is still speaking today! The inclusion of the Gentiles parallels the inclusion of LGBTQ members today.

---

## Simple/Complex Faith

Once the Christians realized that their witness was global, things got considerably more complicated. Proclaiming the possibility of salvation in this world and the next is truly "good news," but telling people *how* to be saved in ways both theologically consistent and pragmatically coherent is another thing altogether. In fact, one of the church's greatest challenges, then and now, is to explain how the objective idea that "God so loved the world" finds its way into the lives and hearts of specific individuals. Clearly, the earliest Christians believed that they had encountered the risen Christ and that the kingdom of God was at hand.

To believe in Jesus was to be "reconciled to God," receive forgiveness of sins, and gain entrance into a new community, the church. Those who accepted the Jesus Way were energized by gospel ideas and action, even when martyrdom loomed large. Soon, however, Christian communities were compelled to develop processes or procedures for presenting persons the faith, instructing them, and, when necessary, disciplining them for inappropriate behavior and belief. Then, as now, some people sustained the faith, while others relinquished, betrayed, or reinterpreted it considerably. Very quickly, Christian churches were forced to define (and divide over) the process of believing, the standards for entry into the church, and the boundaries defining appropriate faith and action.

Becoming a Christian was at once simple and complex. Second-century theologian Justin the Martyr said plainly: "As many as are persuaded and believe that the

THE DEACON

Note to self:
Sermon series titled
"Simplex Faith."

things are true which are taught by us and said to be true, and undertake to be able to live accordingly, are instructed to pray and to entreat God with fasting, for the remission of their past sins." Then, Justin says, they are taken "where there is water, and are born again."[2] Yet Tertullian, his contemporary, was quick to warn that such faith required separation from worldly ideas. He demanded to know, "What is there in common between Athens and Jerusalem?" And concluded: "After Christ Jesus we desire no subtle theories, no acute enquiries after the gospel."[3] Getting into the church was relatively simple; staying in was another matter altogether.

## Faith and Baptism: Where Salvation Begins

Baptism was the door to the church, by which the convert identified with Jesus who himself received the rite in River Jordan. For the early Christians, the question was less "Does baptism save you?" than "Can you really be saved without it?" In other words, faith and baptism were inseparable from the process of salvation.

Again, the *Didache* (110) illustrates the centrality of baptism, its normative mode, and the possibility of logistical exceptions. As the *Didache* describes it, baptism was to be administered "in [cold] running water." But, "if thou hast not running water, baptize in other water [yuck]. If not in cold, then in warm." And if only a little water was available, then "pour water thrice upon the head" in the name of Father, Son, and Spirit.[4] The second-century baptismal norm was immersion in cold, running water. If that was not possible, other options were as valid. Baptism was essential; the mode was negotiable.

THE DEACON

A missionary told a story to my college FCA group where he was "bringing the Word to the deepest part of Africa" and after casting out some demons a man wanted to get baptized before the demons came back with friends. Since they didn't have much water, the missionary got all the saved people to spit in his hand and proceeded to use it on the man's forehead on behalf of the Father, Son, and Holy Spirit.

By the second and third centuries, the process of conversion and baptism was formalized significantly. Only the baptized received the "full service" of the church's worship, preaching, and Eucharistic gifts. The unbaptized catechumens (learners) were those who had professed faith but were required to participate in the extensive training/teaching program that prepared them for the baptismal ritual. The catechumens joined with the congregation for preaching and prayers, but were not permitted to remain for the celebration of the Lord's Supper, a rite limited to the baptized. Life in the catechumenate could extend for up to three years. The baptized were themselves subject to continued evaluation and possible discipline for behaviors and beliefs deemed inappropriate, particularly the "big three" transgressions: adultery, apostasy, or murder.

## Baptism: Getting Naked

By the fourth century, the rituals that moved persons toward baptism were well established, with specific instruction given to the catechumen, a process intensified during the season of Lent, the six weeks before Easter. For many years the baptismal event occurred primarily on Holy Saturday, or during the Easter sunrise observances. In those settings, the candidates entered the baptistery naked as an outward and visible sign of their "new birth." Now that would perk up a Sunday-morning service! (Actually, it was all done decently and in order.) Writing around 350 Cyril of Jerusalem wrote: "as soon, then, as you entered [the baptistery], you put off your tunic; and this was an image of *putting off the old man with his deeds* (Col. 3:9). Having stripped yourselves, you were naked; in this also imitating Christ, who was stripped naked on the Cross. . . ."[5]

---

Sometimes even a bishop like me is glad our liturgy evolved!

**THE BISHOP**

---

On entering the water, individuals might be asked one or more questions such as "Do you believe in God the

Father almighty, and in Jesus Christ his only Son our Lord?" The candidates then responded, "*Credo*," meaning "I believe," and were immersed or had water poured over them in the name of Father, Son, and Holy Spirit. When they came out of the water the newly baptized donned white robes, which were worn for a time as a sign of cleansing and new life. The bishop was always present for these events, linking them to the authority of Christ and the apostles.

---

THE DEACON

Hmm. . . . I have an idea that could double rebaptisms at youth camp.

---

## Deathbed Baptism: Hedging Your Eternal Bets

By the fourth century, as the question of post-baptismal sin became more pronounced, and the regenerative power of baptism more essential, many individuals chose to defer baptism to their deathbeds, or as close to death as possible. If baptism was the outward link to eternal salvation, then best to take no chances of losing it and dying apostate. As we might expect, this was particularly helpful to politicians, the military, and those who just wanted to hedge their bets on eternity. Perhaps the most famous example of that practice was the Emperor Constantine, who postponed his baptism until literally on his deathbed in the year 337. Controversial to the bitter end, Constantine received that baptism at the hands of Eusebius the bishop of Nicomedia, an Arian leader who was excommunicated by the Council of Nicaea. Constantine was nobody's fool; best to cover all the theological bases, just in case the Arians turned out to be right!

## Infant Baptism: Curing the Curse of Original Sin (but Not the Terrible-Twos)

The fourth-century church also made infant baptism increasingly normative, administered as an antidote to the curse of original sin, a sacrament of grace welcoming newborns into the world, and a safeguard for eternity in a time of high infant mortality. As promulgated by Augustine, baptism not only washed away the curse of original sin, it also restored the image of God lost in the fall of Adam and Eve. It was a "regenerating" act inseparably linking divine grace with the water by which it was conveyed.

## Baptism and the State: Citizenship and Salvation

After Constantine, and with the rise of the Christian state across medieval Europe, Christianity became the established, official religion of certain countries, increasing the connection between baptism and citizenship. Over time, to be born into a Christian country required baptism into the Christian church, whatever the majority form—Catholic, Orthodox, Lutheran, Reformed, Anglican—might be. Deviation from that norm was both heresy in the church and treason in the state. Dissenters would suggest that this union of state and church was a form of coerced faith, an imposition of false salvation on an entire people.

THE ACOLYTE

Once the State becomes an expanding empire, this arrangement gets worse. I still have a hard time understanding why people thought this was a good idea.

## Baptism and the Reformation

In their break with Rome, the big three reformers, Martin Luther, John Calvin, and Ulrich Zwingli, retained infant baptism as the door to salvation and the church. Because they connected baptism and citizenship, between an official religion and the public magistrates, they are known as the Magisterial Reformers.

For Martin Luther, baptism was essential for infants, regenerating them by faith. Yes, Luther believed that infants had enough "mustard seed" faith to enable them to draw near to Christ in baptism. However, he asserted that as the entry to faith, in baptism it was less that we chose Christ, than that Christ has chosen us. Baptism marks the little one as Christ's and snatches them from the clutches of Satan. Luther, who loved paradox, wrote: "For (as we have said) even though infants did not believe, which however, is not the case, yet their baptism as now shown would be valid, and no one should rebaptize them."[6] Faith was not necessary, but it was present nonetheless.

For John Calvin and Ulrich Zwingli, baptism was a sign of the covenant between God and God's people.

Baptism was to the New Covenant in Christ what circumcision was to the Covenant with Moses and Abraham. It was offered to the children of the faithful believers who were claimed for the covenant. It was effective, however, meaning it took effect only for those who were among the elect, chosen by God before the foundation of the world. Since only God knows who is elected to salvation and who is not, the church offered baptism as commanded, knowing that it would be appropriate for the saved, while the totally depraved would neither benefit from it nor care. John Calvin suggested that since circumcision was the sign of election and covenant under the old law, it was continued in baptism under the new law. He wrote, "But if the covenant remains firm and fixed, it is no less applicable to the children of Christians in the present day, than to the children of the Jews under the Old Testament."[7]

---

Growing up in the Free Church tradition, the Protestant parsing on baptism always seemed pretty insignificant.

THE DEACON

---

## The Radicals: A Believer's Church

Perhaps the most radical of the Reformation responses to baptism came from the so-called *wiedertaufer* (rebaptizers) or Anabaptists of the sixteenth century and the Baptists of the seventeenth century. These groups constituted various forms of what became known as the Believers' Church, the idea that those who claimed membership in the church must be able to testify to an experience of God's grace through Jesus Christ. Believer's baptism followed that confession of faith. The Anabaptists eschewed infant baptism because they could not find evidence of it in the New Testament, and because infants had no choice in the entry into faith. Baptism was administered after profession of faith rather than before confirmation of faith. This approach was a rejection of the relationship between citizenship and baptism as a form of coerced faith unbecoming to the true gospel. At the same time, the Anabaptists—Swiss Brethren, Mennonites, Hutterites—and Baptists—Particular, General, Six Principle, and Seventh Day, etc.—were often seen as both heretical and treasonous in their relationship to the orthodox church and state.

These believers' churches also varied in the mode of baptism. Some Mennonites, for example, practiced affusion, pouring water on the head three times in the name of Father, Son, and Spirit. Some Mennonites and later Baptists came to practice baptism by immersion, the dipping of the entire body into water, also with the Trinitarian formula. By the 1630s, baptism by immersion became normative for Baptists, and it remains so to this day.

Baptism is the door to the church. Throughout Christian history it has carried multiple forms and multiple theologies. Yet in each of those traditions, baptism is a powerful means or sign of God's grace, the continuing link between sinners and Jesus of Nazareth, crawling into River Jordan, "to fulfill all righteousness."

THE ELDER

My Baptist neighbors are obnoxious about this. They go on and on about John the BAPTIST, kiddie sprinkling, and New Testament Christianity. I am pretty sure they think the planet lost Christianity for 1,500 years!

## Eating and Drinking with Jesus: The Table and the Church

If baptism marks Christian beginnings, the Lord's Supper—Holy Communion, Eucharist—marks the journey. If baptism is a one-time, unrepeated rite in most Christian communions, the Lord's Supper is an enduring spiritual experience for the faithful. The New Testament church clearly used the practice and the language of the Supper to describe the nature of Christian faith and to mark it as a continuing event by which members drew near to Christ and to one another.

Among early Christian authors, the words of the Lord's Supper were direct and literal, although the precise meaning of those words was yet to be defined. Christians spoke of "feeding on Christ," of the bread as his body and the wine as his blood. Justin Martyr wrote that in the second-century church, "This food is called among us 'Eucharist,'" and noted that none were permitted to receive it save those "who believe the things we teach are true, and who has been washed with the washing that is for remission of sins and unto a second birth, and who is so living as Christ has enjoined."[8] From the earliest days the church understood the Table of Christ as space for grace, a sign of salvation. Over time, the church gathered round Christ's table, but with very different interpretations as to the meaning of those simple words, "This is my body; this is my blood."

## Transubstantiation: Feeding on Christ, Literally

The Catholic doctrine of transubstantiation unites multiple elements of Christian doctrine and practice, including biblical literalism, mystical presence, apostolic authority, and direct encounter with the Divine. Indeed, transubstantiation offers a dramatically tangible response to the question of how the idea of God's love and care for humanity becomes a personal experience within the individual Christian. Biblically, the doctrine offers a literal interpretation of the words of Jesus, "This is my Body. This is my blood," and his admonition in John 6:54: "Those who eat my flesh and drink my blood have eternal life and I will raise them up in the last day."

Philosophically, transubstantiation centers in Aristotelian realism, the idea that the eternal is made known in the material; that "things in themselves" contain elements of the transcendent. In this case, by the authority of Christ passed on through the apostles, a duly ordained priest mediates a miracle by which, at the words of institution, "this is my body, this is my blood," the bread and the wine are transformed into the very body and blood of Jesus

Christ. The *accidents* or appearance of bread and wine remain the same, but their *substance* or reality is changed into Christ's very flesh and blood. It looks and tastes like bread and wine, but it's actually Christ himself, entering the soul and body of the baptized individual. Each time the Eucharist (the Mass) is celebrated, Christ is offered again on Calvary for the sins of the world. Thus Christians can know that the presence of the risen Christ has literally come into them. In this way the eternal enters the earthly. Sinful individuals can know that they have tangibly received the risen Christ into themselves. It is indeed a brilliant concept and practice for bridging divine/human gulf, the ultimate and continuing experience of salvation.

---

Wow. That is (symbolically) powerful. I think more Catholics need a little lesson on Aristotle.

THE ELDER

---

It took a while for this powerful doctrine to become official in the church. Conversations, speculations, and debates over transubstantiation evolved over a long period of time, particularly between the ninth and thirteenth centuries. Official approval was not secured until 1215 in the Fourth Lateran Council. It drew on the theology of the great scholastic theologian Thomas Aquinas, who wrote quite simply that by the power of God, "the whole substance of bread is converted into the whole substance of

Christ's body."[9] Transubstantiation tangibilifies grace. It assures Christians that Christ himself has literally come into them. Amid the "troubles of the world," it is a right helpful doctrine.

## Grace for the Journey: The Seven Sacraments

Within certain segments of Christianity, baptism and the Lord's Supper became the centerpieces of a sacramental understanding of salvation and the means of grace. Sacraments are outward and visible signs of inward and spiritual grace, and they occupy a spiritual dimension beyond symbol in connecting individuals to the presence of God. The symbol *represents*; the sacrament *participates* in the grace it conveys. Peter Lombard, the twelfth-century bishop whose four-volume *Book of Sentences* became a standard theological text, was perhaps the first to list seven sacraments by which God's grace is mediated to baptized Christians. These included:

- Baptism: administered to infants (and adults); destroys the curse of original sin; regenerates the heart; the entry point to salvation. (Water is the outward sign.)
- Confirmation: When the faith pledged at baptism becomes the faith of the believing individual. (Oil is the outward sign.)
- Eucharist: The continuing experience of Christ's literal presence; the repetition of "the sacrifice of the mass"; and a literal encounter with Christ physically and spiritually. (Bread and wine are the outward signs.)

- Penance/Confession: A response to the struggle with post-baptismal sin through "auricular confession" to a priest who offers absolution and requires acts of restitution. (The priest offering absolution on Christ's authority is the outward sign.)
- Holy Orders: A vocational choice for a life of service in the church as priests or "religious" monastic men and women. ("Solemn vows" are the outward and visible signs.)
- Marriage: Another vocational choice related to the formation of a Christian family. ("Marriage vows" are the outward and visible sign.)
- Anointing of the Sick/Last Rites: The grace provided when one departs this world. (Oil is the outward sign.)

Meeting in the 1560s, the Council of Trent, responding to doctrinal challenges set forth by Protestant Reformers, declared in no uncertain terms that "[i]f any one saith, that the sacraments of the New Law are not necessary *unto salvation*," or "that, without them men obtain of God, through faith alone, let him be anathema."[10]

## Martin Luther: The "Real Presence" of Christ

Martin Luther, of course, disagreed. Luther rejected transubstantiation, calling it "an invention of human reason . . . based neither on Scripture nor sound reasoning," and insisting that it was built on magic and superstition. He denied that the bread and the wine of the Eucharist were literally transformed into Christ's body and blood, but steadfastly insisted that Christ was truly present both physically and spiritually in those elements since, after the resurrection, because he was "in all things, of all things, and through all things." He was particularly present at the Table, because he promised to be. Likewise, the validity of the sacrament was conditioned upon the faith of the recipients.

This idea of "real presence" separated Luther from other Reformers as evident at the Marburg Colloquy in 1529. There the representatives of various segments of the Reformation agreed on multiple dogmas, but differed considerably over the nature of Holy Communion. Luther himself became so frustrated that he was said to have scrawled "This is my body" across the table and stormed out of the room. Luther often stormed out of rooms.

## The Reformed Tradition: A Spiritual Presence

Both Ulrich Zwingli and John Calvin denied the real physical presence of Christ in the elements, reasoning that since Jesus physically ascended into heaven and was present "at God's right hand," he could in no sense be physically present in the bread and wine. Rather, both affirmed the spiritual presence of Christ at the Table, although to varying degrees.

Zwingli stressed the memorial nature of Holy Communion, evident in Jesus's own command: "Do this in remembrance of me." Thus, as members of the gathered congregation remembered Christ's death and resurrection for the sins of the world, the faith of the individual and the believing community drew nearer to God and to each other. Christ's presence was less evident in bread and wine than in the faith of the believers, who recalled his life and death together at the Table. Of the spiritual benefits of the Supper, Zwingli wrote that it is "necessary and helpful in no small way, for the spiritual memory of the death of Christ, to strengthen the faith and brotherly loyalty, for improving life, and for protecting Christians from vices of their own heart."[11]

---

**THE DEACON**

My Baptist ethics professor got worked up in class once and raised his voice and shook his fist saying, "Jesus said 'Do this in *remembrance* of me!' NOT 'DO ME'!"

---

Zwingli added something of an egalitarian shift to the celebration of the Supper, removing the altar from Zurich's Grossmünster and replacing it with a simple communion table facing and on the same level as the congregation. Participants received both the bread and wine, and were permitted to pass the bread to each other rather than receive it at the hands of a priest or minister.[12]

In a sense, Zwingli memorialized Jesus out of the bread and wine and into the hearts and minds of confessing Christians. His approach to communion is normative in many contemporary congregations today.

John Calvin, on the other hand, gave greater emphasis to a special spiritual presence of Christ experienced when the bread and wine are consecrated and shared in the community of faith. Christ was spiritually present when the Supper was shared, a special "means of grace" in which Christ himself promised to abide with faithful believers. For Calvin, "the sacred mystery of the Supper" consisted in two aspects: "the corporeal signs, presented to the eye," which represented "spiritual things adapted" to our need for visible assurance; and "spiritual truth, which is at once figured and exhibited by the signs."[13]

Anglicans (Episcopalians) developed a classic *via media* (middle way) that liturgically permitted the faithful to come to the Table and take their choice as to what it meant. The *Book of Common Prayer* opens the door and the options with this fascinating rubric: "Eat this bread, remembering that Christ has died for you [memorial?] feeding on Him [real presence?], in your heart [spiritual presence], by faith [multiple options?], with thanksgiving [Eucharist?]." That sixteenth-century confession may be the genius of Anglican efforts to allow for multiple ways of interpreting the Supper, while making it central to the life of both the church and the individual Christian.

---

THE BISHOP

Ah. Moderation. Even my postmodern friends can appreciate the poetic multiplicity within the Book of Common Prayer.

---

## Protestants and Conversion: Once or Twice Born?

When Protestants left transubstantiation and real presence behind, they confronted a new dilemma: How will sinners know that the grace of God has found them, or that they have found God's grace? It was a serious crisis, again related to the way in which the concept of God's love for all humanity could be realized in the lives of specific individuals.

## *The Once-Born: Growing Up in Grace*

Some Christian communions continued what William James called the "once-born" approach for entering into faith, whereby persons were nurtured through the sacramental life of the church. Once-born individuals were welcomed into the world by baptism as infants, nurtured in the life and rituals of the church through childhood, and often affirmed that they had never really known a time when they were not aware of God's love and grace, as experienced through the community of faith.

William James suggested that once-born persons "see God, not as a strict Judge . . . but as the animating spirit of a beautiful harmonious world, Beneficent and Kind, Merciful as well as Pure."[14] He rightly connected this way of salvation with the sacramental tradition of Roman Catholicism and Eastern Orthodoxy, but it is also a significant element within the Lutheran, and Anglican/Episcopal communions. Truth is, most Christian groups make room for a once-born option for individuals who, nurtured in Christian families and churches, grow up to confess that "I always knew that Jesus loved me and was present in my life."

## *The Twice-Born: Conversion and Transformation*

For many Protestant traditions, however, the entry point of faith came through a conversion experience of

God's grace, a "twice-born," decisive religious encounter with the Divine. In his *Varieties of Religious Experience*, James wrote that, "To be converted, to be regenerated, to receive grace, to experience religion, to gain assurance, are so many phrases which denote the process, gradual or sudden, by which a self hitherto divided, and consciously . . . unhappy, becomes unified and . . . happy, in consequence of its firmer hold on religious realities."[15] One still had to "feed on Christ," but the experience was in many ways more inward and less tangible than when one actually ate his flesh and drank his blood in the Eucharistic event.

The concern for individual conversion was not new in Christianity. Paul's Damascus Road experience remains one of the great conversion testimonies of the church's history. Numerous early prominent Christians testified to similar transforming conversions, including Augustine of Hippo, Julian of Norwich, Teresa of Avila, John of the Cross, Martin Luther, John Wesley, Blaise Pascal, Philip Jacob Spener, and many others. The spiritual experiences of these individuals represented something of the mystical tradition of Christianity, direct encounters of the soul with God, often involving ecstatic moments involving visions, voices, and varying revelations. Augustine charts his agonizing quest for conversion, a journey that finally ends when he discovers "a light as it were of serenity infused into my heart." While such dramatic spiritual encounters consistently occurred, they were not a required experience for entrance into the church and did not become normative until relatively late in the church's history.

The Believers' Church advocates—Anabaptists, Baptists, Disciples of Christ—were strong supporters of the

---

I have evangelical friends who can't understand being a Christian without being "born again." When I realized this it seemed odd, but prior I assumed it had something to do with being pro-life.

**THE ACOLYTE**

---

need for conversion in all who claimed membership in Christ's church. The Amsterdam Confession of the earliest Baptists, noted earlier, defined the church in conversionistic terms as "a company of faithful people separated from the world by the word & Spirit of GOD . . . being knit unto the LORD, & one unto another, by Baptism . . . upon their own confession of faith . . . and sins."[16] Conversion brought with it a change of heart and life, oriented away from self and sin, and toward Christ and Christian discipleship. It was the entrance to salvation for "new life" in this world, and eternal life in the next.

## Getting Saved: Multiple Plans

### *Calvinists: Total Depravity—Limited Atonement*

In both England and America, as the need for conversion became increasingly important to large groups of ministers and congregations, revivals became a mechanism for reaching sinners with the gospel and encouraging them to experience redemption for themselves. The debate, however, centered in *who* could be saved, and *how* it was possible. Those who identified themselves as Calvinists confronted Arminians over the nature of conversion and who was a necessary candidate for redemption.

Calvinists suggested that salvation was necessary because all persons were totally depraved as a result of the fall of Adam and Eve and could in no way save themselves. All deserved damnation and eternal punishment, but God in sovereign mercy had chosen some (the elect) for salvation and provided the means for doing that in the death and resurrection of Jesus Christ. That God should elect even some persons unconditionally for salvation was an undeserved gift. The elect might ignore or resist grace, but ultimately it was irresistible to them. Thus Christ's death on the cross applied only for the sins of the elect; it was a "limited" atonement. All the elect would be saved; but only the elect would be saved. God alone knew who was in each camp.

## Arminians: Free Will—General Atonement

Jacob Arminius, seventeenth-century Dutch Calvinist, offered an alternative reading of the process and effects of salvation. He insisted that all persons were potentially elected but were actually saved when they met the terms of election: repentance and faith. Human nature was depraved, true enough, but retained enough prevenient, or enabling, grace to permit us to choose or reject the gift of salvation. God's saving grace cooperated with the enabling grace within each person, thereby accomplishing redemption for all who chose to believe. Later on,

Arminians suggested that if persons had the free will to move toward the new birth they also had the free will to turn away from it. Falling from grace, a conscious decision to reject the grace one had once received, was a real possibility. Believers should persevere through sanctification, and the grace of Christian living.

These views of the nature of salvation became part of the theology of conversion set forth by various Protestant groups, and became trajectories for faith commitments. Conversion became a normative entry point for a segment of Christians who came to be known as evangelicals. Revivals in Britain led to the so-called Wesleyan Awakening of the eighteenth century, and in America the First and Second Great Awakenings of the eighteenth and nineteenth centuries. Later on, revivals became an evangelistic tool for encouraging mass conversions around the world, extending to Christian groups in Asia, Africa, and South America. Revival meetings, public gatherings to renew Christian spirituality or lead the unconverted to faith, became a popular means for conversions. Calvinist preachers urged sinners to wait for God to infuse grace into the hearts of the elect, while Arminians called for immediate conversion of sinners through exercise of their free will. Pentecostals moved through conversion to a "second baptism" of the Holy Spirit.

Revivals created a new group of religious leader/celebrities, from Jonathan Edwards preaching to colonial "sinners in the hands of an angry God," to nineteenth-century evangelists like Charles Finney and D. L. Moody demanding instantaneous conversion of all, to Billy Sunday, Aimee Semple McPherson, Billy Graham, and Oral Roberts holding mass crusades in America and across the world, to twenty-first-century preachers like T. D. Jakes, Creflo Dollar, Joyce Myer, and Joel and Victoria Osteen, some of whom linked conversion to material prosperity.[17]

## Pentecostals: Thrice-Born Holiness

There's a great story from the 1950s concerning a distinguished evangelical seminary professor lecturing on the Pentecostal phenomenon sweeping large segments of the church. After the professor's rather strong critique of the movement, a student raised a hand. "So, professor, after all you've said do you think there will be any Pentecostals in heaven?" "Yes," he responded, "if they don't overshoot it!"

---

THE DEACON

I use to speak in tongues and now this topic just makes me uncomfortable. My Jewish therapist told me my embarrassment is about my parents more than the Holy Spirit.

---

Pentecostalism, one of the twentieth and early twenty-first century's fastest-growing movements, began as a minority, largely on the economic and ecclesiastical margins. Pentecostal approaches to salvation moved through a twice-born conversionism to a thrice-born emphasis on the baptism of the Holy Spirit, evidenced by speaking in tongues (glossolalia). This post-conversion experience was the sign of sanctification and holiness, carrying the believer to a continuous life in the Spirit. For Pentecostals, the restoration of the Pentecost anointing began in the year 1901, in Topeka, Kansas, when a holiness teacher named Charles Fox Parham encouraged his students to pray for a revival evidenced by the baptism of the Holy Spirit. On New Year's Eve, 1901, a woman named Agnes Ozman experienced such a baptism, and, observers said, began to speak in the Chinese language. A similar outpouring occurred in 1906 in Los Angeles at the Azusa Street mission led by an African American named William Seymour. The movement burgeoned across North America and soon went global, with strong congregations established in Asia, Africa, and South America. Pentecostals were "Holy Ghosters" and "Holy Rollers," given to a variety of frenzied "enthusiasms," on which they claimed an arresting encounter with the Holy Spirit.

---

**THE ELDER**

My granddaughter is a Doctor and Charismatic. She always points out how much more diverse her congregation is than my parish. She has a point, but I can't manage to tell her I'm just a curmudgeon.

---

Pentecostalism was closely related to the earlier Holiness movement, a revival-based emphasis on

Spirit-baptism as the vehicle for continued cleansing from sin and sanctification for holy living. Pentecostals simply formalized such Spirit baptism by linking it to the experience of tongues and healing as signs of spiritual empowerment. This experience was a powerful equalizer. It was "poured out on all flesh," regardless of gender, race, or economic status. Women could be called to preach as readily as men; those without formal education or economic resources could be overtaken by divine revelation. At Azusa Street, William Seymour declared that the "color line" was washed away in the "blood of the Lamb." By the twenty-first century, Pentecostalism reflected a global constituency, Korean churches with hundreds of thousands of attendees, to South American house churches, to tongues-speaking, hand-raising American Presbyterians![18]

## The Twenty-First Century: A Conversion Crisis?

Pentecostalism is one example of the continuing global impact of the Christian message, even as Christianity in the West struggles amid the rise of the religiously unaffiliated "nones," and the disengagement of many Christians from full participation in church life. This disconnect has created something of a conversion crisis across the theological and denominational spectrum, particularly in North America and Europe. Once-born churches depend on families who bring their children into the nurturing grace of the sacraments early in life. Twice-born churches depend on awakening sinners to their need of salvation and the experience of a conversion to new life and church membership. As fewer people respond to that message, twice-born churches confront their own crisis of identity and methodology for declaring the gospel. This crisis seems to have driven many Christian individuals and churches back to the Jesus Story, rethinking its meaning and its application in societies where Christianity has lost or is fast losing culture-privilege. Analysts like the Philip Jenkins see these transitions as signs of a "global Christianity" that "can make us see the whole religion in a radically new perspective" at once "startling and, often, uncomfortable." Thus the church is compelled to rethink and restate the plan of salvation, "not just for what it is, but what it was in its origins and what it is going to be in the future."[19]

Through it all, the unpredictability of the Spirit remains. I learned that the Sunday that our daughter Stephanie and I received Holy Communion at a Lutheran Church in Richmond, Kentucky, her first time to join the Lutherans at Christ's Table. She was ahead of me in the line, received the bread, ate it, and then took a sip from the cup, her first taste of Real Presence and real wine. Immediately she turned to me and asked: "Dad, what was that?" "It's the Spirit, Stephanie," I replied. "The Holy Spirit." One can only hope.

6

# "Salt Me Well, Salt Me Well": Dissent as a Signpost in Christian History

Oh salt me well, brothers, salt me well." That's how Balthasar Hubmaier, doctor of theology, Anabaptist preacher, and one-time priest, is said to have counseled his Catholic executioners on March 10, 1528, when they sprinkled sulfur and gunpowder into his "rather long" beard to hasten his dying on the medieval stake. Imprisoned in Austria in 1527, Hubmaier and his spouse, Elizabeth Hugline Hubmaier, were condemned for their repudiation of infant baptism and affirmation of a believers' church. Though tortured, he refused to recant, a dissenter to the end. "Fixed like an immovable rock in his heresy," one observer noted. Elizabeth Hubmaier also refused recantation and was drowned in River Danube three days after her husband's execution.[1]

The Hubmaiers' heretical dissent was considerable. They dismissed infant baptism as a sign of governmentally coerced faith with no precedent in the New Testament, while insisting that the church should be composed only of believers, those who could testify to an experience of grace for themselves, as symbolized in believer's baptism. (Their very marriage represented a breach of Balthasar's priestly vows of celibacy.) Worse yet, Balthasar Hubmaier was one of the earliest Reformation leaders to advocate for religious liberty as essential for both a healthy state and a free church. He even supported liberty of conscience for heretic and unbeliever alike; God alone was judge of conscience. That bit of dissent set him at odds with Catholics and most Protestants. Yet Hubmaier was unrelenting: governmentally coerced faith and baptism wasn't much faith at all. For that dissenting principle, the Hubmaiers were willing to die.

---

**THE ELDER**

Anyone willing to die nonviolently because of a conviction is inspiring. Personally I think I would have told the executioners about my high blood pressure rather than requesting more salt.

---

Balthasar laid out those views in 1524 in a treatise whose title became his epitaph: *Concerning Heretics and those who Burn them*. At a time when almost no one could have imagined it, Hubmaier opened the door to what became modern religious freedom, conscience uncoerced by state or established church. Church-state dynamics represent one of the saddest though ultimately promising sagas in Christian history.

## Dissent in America: Muhammad Ali Style

On November 17, 1999, I met Muhammad Ali. It was at the Cathedral of the Assumption on Fifth Street in Louisville, Kentucky, during a Cathedral Heritage Series of ecumenical gatherings. I was the preacher for an interfaith Thanksgiving Service, and Muhammad Ali was receiving a lifetime service award for assorted humanitarian activities in his hometown and beyond.

Just being there was a poignant moment. The Cathedral, built in 1850, was the scene of Bloody Monday, August 6, 1855, that infamous day of Protestant-generated anti-Catholic, anti-immigrant riots in which some twenty people were killed. In 1855, no one in Louisville, Protestant or Catholic, would have envisioned an interfaith service in that venerable Catholic sanctuary, in which a Baptist preached and an African American Muslim received an interfaith award.

That night, I arrived at the newly renovated Cathedral in the company of my great friend Father Clyde Crews, Louisville native and Bellarmine University professor. Since we were early, Clyde suggested we slip into the sacristy at the back of the church. And there, leaning against the sacristy wall, stood Muhammad Ali. The shock of seeing him up close took our collective breaths away. Without thinking, I extended my hand, and murmured haltingly,

"Mr. Ali, you've been a hero for me a long time." Muhammad Ali smiled, and without a word, leaned down, and *kissed me on the cheek*. It was a split-second, time-marking moment etched in my memory.

The memory of those events swept over me on June 10, 2016, as we watched Ali's memorial service, at once a local and international celebration of the breadth of his faith, the strength of his character, and the joy of his compassion. Secure in his Muslim faith, Ali left this world amid an array of voices that included Baptist pastor Kevin Cosby, politically radical rabbi Michael Lerner, Native American and Buddhist holy men, a student intern, the endearingly hilarious Billy Crystal, and former President Bill Clinton. Indeed, the service was a paean to American religious-ethnic-racial diversity and dissent; a witness against racist rhetoric and bad religion that all too easily rears its ugly head here and now.

Ali was one of the most public religio-political dissenters in late twentieth-century America, renouncing his "slave name," Cassius Clay, for the Islamic Muhammad Ali; refusing to register for the draft in opposition to the Vietnam War; having his boxing championship title revoked; and being sentenced to five years in prison. (The title was ultimately restored, and the prison sentence removed.) Ali took a chance on Islam, not knowing where it would take him, but believing it offered a freedom that the Christianity of the segregationist South could not. Perhaps Rev. Cosby said it for all of us who gamble on grace and engage in dissent for conscience sake: "You have to bet on the Derby horse while it's in the mud, not the winner's circle." Perhaps that's the chance dissenters have to take.[2]

## Dissent in the Christian Community: Mixed Blessings

Religious dissent in its varied theological, political, and personal forms runs like a thread of blood, sweat, and tears through the history of the Christian church. It is reflected in the voices of preachers, martyrs, heretics, mystics, and clairvoyants who claimed revelations ranging from deep spiritual insights to the downright bizarre—sometimes from the same people! Those folks and their challenges to order and uniformity in church and state represent communities of dissent present in the church's past, present, and future. Along the way, dissent invigorates the church even as it disrupts it. When the dictionary defines dissent as "to publicly disagree with an official opinion, decision, or set of beliefs," it describes large segments of Christianity then and now.[3]

The church began in a crisis with the state. Jesus of Nazareth was executed at the hands of the Romans. His followers were convinced he rose from the dead, but with the exception of a centurion or two, yet another dying and rising god didn't make much of an impression on the Romans. (The mystery religions of the day were thick with dying and rising deities.)

And it didn't take long for things to get all first-century-litigious. In the famous Philippian Jailer story of Acts 17, Paul and Silas were thrown in prison for preaching the gospel, beaten, and left in chains in the "innermost cell." An earthquake broke open the prison doors, but Paul and Silas stayed put. The jailer, astounded that no one escaped, believed in Jesus. He and his entire family were baptized on the spot. Next morning, the magistrates bid the jailer to turn them loose, but Paul would have none of it, reminding their handlers that they were publicly beaten, and jailed without a trial. "And now," he asked (sounding like a first-century ACLU lawyer), "they are going to discharge us in secret? Certainly not!" He waited on the magistrates themselves to make amends. So the magistrates, afraid when they discovered that Paul and Silas were Roman citizens, "came and apologized" (Acts 16:35–39). Apparently Paul took advantage of his Roman status for as long as he could, consistently appealing to Rome when his civil rights were violated. Ultimately, his case was finally "settled" with his execution. If it looked as if Rome had the upper hand, the writer of Revelation thought otherwise: "Then I saw a new heaven and a new earth; for the first heaven and the first earth had passed away . . ." (Revelation 21:1).

## Religious Dissent: An Inevitable Necessity

Internal dissent was present in the church from the beginning, challenging majoritarian views, offering alternative readings to Scripture, unsettling efforts to develop "normative" theology and practice. Indeed, dissent was and remains essential and messy.

In *Dissent in American Religion*, Edwin Scott Gaustad writes, "Should a society actually succeed, however, in suffocating all contrary opinion, then its own vital juices no longer flow and the shadow of death begins to fall across it. No society—ecclesiastical or political, military or literary—can afford to be snared by its own slogans."[4] Gaustad's discussion of the nature of dissent in the U.S. provides insights for the larger church as well. He notes:

> Dissent cannot be understood simply in terms of whines against oppression, resistance to organizational corruption, demurrers against the

> affirmation of others. To view dissent in these terms is to suppose that when all external restraints are removed and all ecclesiastical authority stilled, then dissent falls flat on its face never to rise again. This could be the case only if dissenters were merely noisy nay-sayers. [Instead,] the dissenter is a powerful if unpredictable engine in the service of a cause.

For Gaustad, dissenters reflect an essential element of religion itself, since "religion in its essence is already off beat, irregular, asymmetric."[5] In the larger sense, dissent "may also be a manifestation of the unfettered human spirit."[6] Dissent and dissenters are messy. They may also be the church's best conscience.

---

Yes! I love how generations later we eventually get around to celebrating and honoring dissenters. The challenge is not to tame them in our retelling.

THE ACOLYTE

---

---

Regarding dissenters, I'm #NotAFan.

THE BISHOP

---

Gaustad's analysis of dissent provides an insightful guide to the church's "strange ones" who push the envelope of dogma and culture with a dissent that is "elusive and erratic"; and "religious dissent, far from being an exception to that rule, is an exaggeration of it." Indeed, he concludes, "True dissent has too many moods, too many guises, too many brief incarnations."[7] Yet Gaustad warns that the "clanging cymbals of consensus" in church and society may shut out dissent or ignore it altogether.[8] This chapter provides illustration of varying aspects of dissent in Christian communions, with particular attention to church/state relationships, and the elusive quest for religious liberty. The role of dissent in Christian history, whether inside or outside the church, cannot be overlooked.

## Martyrdom: The Ultimate Sacrifice

In the early conflicts between the church and the Roman Empire, dissent was inevitably connected to the possibility of martyrdom. Christianity began on the margins of ancient society and stayed there for quite some time. Jesus himself was the ultimate martyr for truth and grace, and others understood themselves to be privileged in following in his footsteps. Persecution created turmoil and shaped identity for the new congregations gathered around Jesus and his way of viewing life.

Early on, Roman civil officials often acted in ways that contributed to the development of a whole school of Christian martyrs, individuals who refused to offer incense at the shrine of the emperor, or who challenged the prevailing religious conventions of first-century,

Roman-dominated society. For Christians, compromise with culture or pagan religious establishments was grounds for apostasy, dismissal from the church in this world and possibly the next. By their great sacrifices—financial, personal, familial—ultimately the sacrifice of their own lives "for the sake of Jesus and the gospel," the martyrs provided a powerful Christian example, dedication, and salvation. Such sacrifice later convinced many that they had a particular eternal relationship with God that had intercessory implications. In other words, they could get through to God like nobody else!

For a couple of centuries, it didn't get much better. Martyrdom became something of a norm in Christian experience, spirituality, and lore. As we have seen, Roman government and Christian theology collided with some frequency, so much so that Tertullian was wont to suggest, *Semen est sanguis Christianorum*, "the Christian's blood is the seed," or better said, "the blood [of the martyrs] is the seed of the Church." From the time of the Emperor Nero (60s CE), there were certain intense periods of persecution, some empire-wide, others regional, particularly under the Emperors Decius (250) and Diocletian (302). Much of the state-based harassment resulted when Christians refused to provide the required offering at the shrine of the Roman emperor, or to turn over holy books when Roman officials confiscated and destroyed the church's sacred texts. Also as noted, these periods of persecution created their own controversies *inside* the church regarding readmission of the *lapsi* (the lapsed), those who had caved in to the imperial requirements, or who turned over holy books, or who were ordained and/or baptized by those who had committed apostasy. All of this ignited perhaps the most far-reaching issue: forgiveness for post-baptismal sins, particularly the "big three" sins of apostasy, adultery, and murder. If you sinned at all, but particularly if you sinned horribly, were you lost to grace? And if so, could you get back in?

## The Cult of Martyrs: Real and Imagined

Widespread persecution began with a vengeance by the year 250, but was present much earlier, brought against those who merely called themselves Christians. Later, Christians came under serious attack for failing to offer sacrifices to the Roman emperors, who were thought to be deities.[9]

Christians really were fed to wild beasts, set aflame, crucified, and beheaded as a result of their explicit or implicit dissent against the state. The martyrs were the earliest mass heroes in the church's history. They were important for many reasons. First, they gave the last full measure of devotion, sacrificing their lives for the sake of their faith. Their sacrifice confirmed the presence and power of God and assured them of salvation. Second, their suffering and death at the hands of the church's adversaries mirrored the suffering and death of Jesus, the church's greatest martyr. Third, their behavior was a source of strength for the church at large, assuring the faithful of the ability to stand firm in other times of trouble. Fourth, ultimately the cult of martyrs became a major element in the cult of the saints, those who had lived so close to Christ that they received a special spiritual status as intercessors on behalf of other, weaker Christian brothers and sisters. After the apostles, the martyrs were the church's first saints, representatives of Christian sacrifice, and spiritual mentors across the generations. Their dissent brought them into conflict with the principalities and powers of this world, and they achieved "a crown of glory."

---

When I graduated high school my youth minister gave me a copy of *Foxe's Book of the Martyrs* to prepare my soul for the persecution that awaits at the university.

THE DEACON

---

Persecution created innumerable stories—martyrologies—of the deaths of the martyrs, stories retold, recorded, and circulated as examples of faithfulness, determination, and a willingness to die rather than deny Christian faith. The literature of martyrs and martyrdom took on its own mythic style and detail, sometimes factual, sometimes a little less so.

The case of Vibia Perpetua, a young mother from North Africa, martyred in 203, illustrates the point. Arrested and jailed, she was brought before the Roman Procurator Hilarianus, who demanded, "Spare your father's gray hairs, spare your infant boy. Offer the sacrifice for the emperor's well-being."

"I will not make it," Perpetua asserted.

The Procurator asked: "Are you a Christian?"

"I am a Christian," she replied. Perpetua was willing to desert her child and family for greater devotion to her faith.[10]

## Constantine: From Martyrdom to Privilege

Then came Constantine, claiming the title of Roman Emperor after his victory over his competitor Maxentius at the Battle of Milvan Bridge, October 28, 312. Eusebius of Caesarea, bishop and church historian, claimed that before the battle Constantine received a vision of the Chi Rho, Greek letters combining the first two letters of *Christus*, with the admonition "in this sign conquer." Emblazing that symbol on the helmets of his soldiers, Constantine's victory precipitated his own appreciation for, if not conversion to, Christianity. As emperor, he extended toleration to various religions in the empire, but he also became engaged in church affairs, sensing that Christianity could become a source of moral guidance and political unity for the huge empire. As noted earlier, Constantine received baptism into Christian faith on his deathbed (deferred baptism is probably a good thing for politicians).

Suddenly the persecuted became the privileged, a status expanded when the Emperor Theodosius I (379–395) chose to promote Christianity as Rome's official state religion. These actions marked a phenomenon that came to be known as Constantinianism, a state-church relationship that took shape in medieval claims that Europe was the church; papal claims of authority over both the secular and spiritual swords; religious establishments throughout Europe and portions of America; and even the present housing allowance tax break for ordained ministers in the US of A. The term Constantinian may involve any special relationship between church and state, implicit or explicit, past and present.

THE BISHOP

Most people don't realize how many legal and tax perks religious communities and leaders get in the U.S. We may not have a state religion, but we have a state-subsidized market for religious entrepreneurs.

## Persecution from Within: The Church against the "Pagans"

As one might expect, some of the persecuted became the persecutors. It started with the pagans. During the time of persecution, individuals such as Justin Martyr (himself a victim of persecution) had referred to "enlightened pagans," or "Christians before Christ," whose religious insights bore a limited but nonetheless profound influence of the divine *logos* that became flesh in Jesus. With their increasing state-privileged status, some Christians turned their attention to the potentially detrimental impact of non-Christian groups.

The term *pagan* was increasingly utilized to describe those outside the church who worshiped false gods. The Latin word *paganus* means simply "rural" or "in the country," so originally, pagans were those who dwelt in the country. By the fourth century, Christians used the term for referring to those rural folk who continued to follow the "ancient idolatry" long after Christianity had caught on in more populated areas.[11] Pagans were those who were "outside the city," or beyond God's orthodox community. Some early Christians like Justin thought certain pagans had divine insight; many later Christians thought they were all going to hit hell wide open.

---

THE DEACON

One of my friends self-identifies as a Pagan Franciscan. I am not exactly sure what it means beyond wearing a rosary during eco-activism.

---

In a treatise titled *On the Error of Profane Religions* (c. 350), Firmicus Maternus, a pagan convert to Christianity, urged the co-emperors Constantius I and Constans to take government action, writing that "these abominations . . . must be extirpated radically, in order to destroy them; apply to them the most severe regulations of your edicts, do not allow the Roman world to be sullied any longer by this disastrous error. . . ."[12] Such is the stuff of which inquisitions are made.

The emperors did not attempt such punitive actions at that time, and apparently many Christians believed that the "rural people" would soon relinquish their more ignorant practices as the Christian gospel gained cultural and spiritual ascendancy. When that did not readily occur, Emperor Theodosius and later "Christian" emperors used certain legal means to do the trick, closing temples, forbidding Christians to reconvert to the old practices, and requiring significant fines for enactment of pagan rituals, particularly blood sacrifices.[13]

## *Corpus Christianum*: Europe as the Church

From the time of Constantine to the unification of Italy in 1870, the church/state relationship in Europe was a religio-political drama of the first order. With the conquest of the barbarian Romans by the various barbarian tribes of northern Europe, the churches, East and West, made their own conquests, sending monks and missionaries to Christianize the French, German, English, Irish, and Slavic peoples. Pope Zachary's recognition of Pepin (Pippin) as King of the Franks in 751 gave Rome an army to protect it and solidified Pepin's less-than-legitimate claim to power in Gaul. The coronation of Pepin's son, Charlemagne, in the year 800, was icing on the church-state cake. And, as we have seen, later popes claimed authority to make and unmake European rulers at will. Sometimes it worked, sometimes it didn't. Being a king or a Catholic in medieval Europe was messy business.

By the ninth and tenth century, church-state relationships meant that Europe essentially *was* the church. To be born into a European "Christian" country was to be baptized into the Christian church, by mandate. Thus, citizenship and baptism were inseparable. Dissent was suspect; treason in the state was heresy in the church and vice versa. This link between the two institutions set the scene for responses to dissent that became a major characteristic of the medieval church.

## The Inquisition: Theological Dissent Meets Social Control

As the early Christian centuries turned into the Middle Ages, the church's response to dissent became more intense and decisive. A variety of individuals pushed back against this type of normative Christianity. The Inquisition evolved into a method for dealing with dissent, often utilizing the twin systems of church and state. Originally, what became the Inquisition was a concern for church discipline, calling out individuals who were outside doctrinal or ethical norms in the churches. Church discipline was perceived as a way of encouraging Christians who had strayed from Christian doctrine or morality back into the good graces of God and the church. But dissenters were another issue. They offered alternative views, doctrines, and biblical interpretations that challenged prevailing dogmas and practices. When these ideas were put forward, often by articulate, charismatic individuals, the leaders of "normative Christianity" feared that the "little ones," weaker Christians who were easily influenced, would be led astray. Protecting them from heretics was a major goal of the Inquisition, but the resulting violence and injustice turned into a form of social control, often against all who implicitly or explicitly dissented against the theological, ecclesiastical, or cultural status quo.

## Medieval Dissent: The Cathari

Medieval Christianity experienced dissenting movements whose beliefs and practices set them over against religious establishments, particularly the Roman papacy.

I use to be against church discipline until church gossip found its way into email. Now I am trying to get the hacker group Anonymous to help me set things to right. LOL

THE BISHOP

The Cathari, or Albigenses, were a twelfth- and thirteenth-century group that formed near the city of Albi, in the area of southwestern France/northern Spain, then known as Languedoc. They challenged Catholic doctrine in multiple ways, denying the validity of the sacraments, the authority of the pope, and the traditional theology of the church. Their intent was to purify Christianity, hence their "cathartic" name and endeavors. The Cathari suggested that the human body was a source of great evil, and that denying the flesh was a way to move toward greater spiritual insight. They replaced Catholic sacraments with a once-for-all ceremony of purification from sin called the *consolamentum*, involving a communal laying on of hands. In fact, their highest form of martyrdom was a rite they called the *endura*, essentially starving oneself to death. They denied the Trinity, affirmed reincarnation, and resisted a hierarchical view of church authority (bishops were out).

The Cathari were public dissenters, not failing to challenge Catholic doctrine in the public square. Their sincerity and the intensity of belief and practice inspired many, so much so that Pope Innocent III instigated a crusade

THE BISHOP

I don't like the sound of this at all! A strict observance group rejected marriage, yet supported contraception. Those *perfecti* were strict vegetarians, refusing to eat anything that was related to the extension of the flesh.

against them in 1208. Church/state dynamics were such that certain French nobles defended the Cathars in reaction against invasion at the behest of an Italian pope. The Cathari were ultimately defeated, however.

## Protestants and the State: "Whose prince, his religion"

The Protestant Reformation complicated that plan, as entire regions of Germany went Lutheran, and an entire country, England, went Anglican. The terrible Thirty Years War (1618–1648), in which a generation of European males was wiped out, was in part a struggle among Catholic, Reformed, and Lutheran regions over power and place. Nonetheless, the religious establishments prevailed with official, privileged churches in various principalities across Europe. For years the principle, *cuius regio, eius religio* (literally "whose prince, his religion") meant that each time a monarch died, the successors were at once affirmed for and endangered by their faith perspective. To unite all of France after the Wars of Religion, the Protestant Henri Bourbon (Henri IV) was required to become a Catholic. He did so, and was crowned king in 1589 with one of the great one-liners of Christian history: "Paris is worth a Mass." Enough said.

---

Could you imagine Presidential Elections if this were the case? At least people would have stopped calling President Obama a Muslim.

THE ELDER

---

Protestant-oriented Elizabeth Tudor became queen of England in 1558, seeking a *via media* between Catholic and Protestant, but it took at least thirty years and the defeat of the Spanish Armada in 1588 before Catholic efforts to overthrow her diminished. Meanwhile, the rise of English Puritanism pushed Anglicans toward greater Protestantization. Church/state tensions over the religion of specific monarchs, the role of religious establishments, and the firm if gradual concern for religious liberty endured for centuries.

## Church, State, and Dissent: The Beginnings of Religious Liberty

In a sense, the Protestant Reformation was a widespread movement of dissent against the Roman Catholic Church and its culture of privileged relationship. Yet for a minority of early Protestants, dissent marked a concern for religious liberty and freedom of conscience for all persons within the state. As we have already noted, however, dissent came to be a distinguishing mark of the so-called Radical Reformation. As noted earlier, the Anabaptist scholar/preacher Balthasar Hubmaier wrote an important treatise titled *Concerning Heretics and those Who burn them*, in which he challenged the idea of Inquisition and the "Christian" execution of theological dissenters (heretics). Balthasar Hubmaier wrote that "it is well and good that the secular authority puts to death the criminals who do physical harm to the defenseless, Romans 13. But no one may injure the atheist who wishes nothing for himself other than to forsake the gospel." Even atheists (atheists!) were free to reject faith altogether without persecution by the state. Hubmaier concluded with the assertion: "Now it is apparent to everyone, even the blind, that the law which demands the burning of heretics is an invention of the Devil. 'Truth is immortal.'"[14] This assertion is one of the earliest claims for religious liberty in Western Europe.

---

THE DEACON

"Truth Is Immortal" would make a sweet tattoo.

---

Dissent related to religious liberty became a major issue in England as new, second-generation Protestant groups—Congregationalists, Baptists, Presbyterians, Quakers, Levelers, Seekers, and other sectarian movements—took shape. With the development of the Anglican Church under Henry VIII and the rise of the sectarians, debates developed on the need for uniformity of belief and practice. By the early 1600s, William Laud, Archbishop of Canterbury, sought to enforce conformity, particularly toward those attempting to purify the Church of England from the "trappings of popery." (These folks were the Puritans of various theological stripes.) Some Puritans, for example, dissented from within the Anglican Church, hoping to reform it in more Protestant directions. Other Puritan Separatists concluded that the C of E was in fact a false church from which true Christians should separate themselves entirely.

In 1609, a group of those English Puritan Separatists, exiled in Amsterdam, formed the first Baptist church ever established in this world. They rejected infant baptism in favor of the baptism of believers, those who could testify to an experience of grace in the heart. The authority of Christ, they believed, was mediated through the congregation of believers. They were advocates of religious liberty, insisting that the requirement to baptize infants constituted an effort to coerce faith as imposed by the English state and its official Anglican Church.

These Baptists knew from the beginning that they were a dissenting community of faith. Their earliest confession of 1611 declared that the community of baptized believers constituted "the Bodie of Christ" and therefore ought to "come together, to Pray, Prophecie, breake bread, and administer in all the holy ordinances, although as yet they have no Officers, or that their Officers should bee in Prison, sick, or by anie other meanes hindered from the Church."[15] In founding early Baptist churches, it was anticipated that the ministers might well be put in prison given the radical nature of their church/state dissent.

It was not until 1689 that an Act of Toleration gave enough space for an "assembly of persons dissenting from the Church of England" to hold their own meetings without harassment from the state. These nonconformist dissenters were required to sign or affirm belief in the doctrine of the Trinity, and pledge allegiance to the English crown. They were also forbidden at any time to have "the doors locked, barred, or bolted, during any time of such meeting together."[16] Such toleration permitted a degree of freedom of worship, but nonconformists were still taxed for support of the Anglican Church. Toleration was a long way from religious freedom.

THE ACOLYTE

I'd go to prison for Jesus.

THE ELDER

I'd visit you.

## The Quest for Freedom, and the Necessity of Dissent

The American experience provides a now-classic case study in the search for freedom in the modern era, not only in the quest for religious liberty, but also regarding the church's role in both the promotion and abolition of chattel slavery. Beyond the mythology that early America was a seedbed of religious liberty is the reality of colonial religious establishments including Puritans in New England and Anglicans in the South. The Puritans who came to Massachusetts Bay in 1630 escaped religious intolerance visited on Protestant nonconformists in England, only to oppose liberty for those who dissented against their particular type of Calvinism. They required church attendance, taxed the populace for the support of the Congregational Church, and brought charges against nonconformists. They insisted that religious uniformity was necessary to undergird the moral and spiritual foundations of a Christian commonwealth. Heretics and dissenters were a threat to that stable social and religious order. (Religiously speaking, Americans are obsessed with sects!)

In the struggle for religious liberty, there were many dissenting voices. Roger Williams, the quintessential dissenter, was a pain in the Puritan religious establishment from the moment he got off the boat from England in 1631. His "erroneous and dangerous" opinions were extensive, including insistence that Native Americans, rather than the King of England, were the real owners of the land and should be compensated appropriately. He was particularly opposed to forcing Christianity on the natives, writing, "Boast not proud English, of thy birth & blood, Thy brother Indian is by birth a Good. Of one blood God made Him, and Thee, & All, As wise, as fair, as strong, as personall."[17]

While he acknowledged that magistrates had civil authority over matters of state, they had no power over souls and salvation. Still worse, Williams insisted that the state could not dictate to the "consciences of the Jews, nor . . . of the Turks or Papists, or Pagans themselves excepted."[18]

For those ideas and his refusal to be silenced about them, Williams was exiled from Massachusetts' "Christian Commonwealth" in the winter of 1636 into the forests of New England. Exile meant he was "denied the common air to breathe in, and a civil cohabitation upon the same common earth; yea and also without mercy and human compassion, exposed to winter miseries in a howling wilderness."[19] For fourteen weeks he wandered, not knowing "what bread or bed did mean." The Narragansett Indians saved him; he bought land from them to found Providence where religious liberty was surprisingly normative.

In describing the Providence colony (and Rhode Island in general) and its own religious radicalism, Williams wrote, "I desired it might be for a shelter for persons distressed for conscience. I then considering the condition of divers of my distressed countrymen, [I] communicated my said purchase unto loving friends . . . who then desired to take shelter here with me."[20] It was a colony, and a church, begun in exile. Rhode Island became a sanctuary for seventeenth-century religious fanatics, dissenters, and theological deviants. Dr. John Clarke, Baptist physician, preacher, and founder of the town of Newport, worked with Williams in writing the charter of the Rhode Island colony. It states, "No person within said colony at any time hereafter shall be in any wise molested, punished, disquieted or called into question for any differences of opinion in matters of religion. . . ."[21] Clarke, Williams, and the Rhode Island charter anticipated not only religious freedom but religious pluralism, born, less because of the Enlightenment, than their concern for conscience and uncoerced faith.

I am sure some of my peers experienced the confirmation process as a subtle form of coercion.

**THE ACOLYTE**

First, they said that faith cannot be compelled. Religious and governmental institutions cannot, must not, impose faith on their citizens. Coerced faith is no faith. Second, these colonial dissenters warned that faith cannot be nationalized. There are no Christian nations, they insisted, only Christian people, bound to Christ, not by citizenship, but by faith. Again, Clarke wrote that no "believer or servant of Jesus Christ hath any liberty, much less authority from his Lord to smite his fellow servant, nor with outward force . . . to constrain, or restrain . . . conscience."[22] The struggle for such liberty of conscience was a long time coming, and not before Quaker preacher Mary Dyer was hanged in Boston; First Baptist Church, Boston, boarded up by state mandate; and Baptist and Quaker preachers beaten in Massachusetts and Virginia.

## Religious Liberty in America: Constitutional and Grudging

By 1791, the First Amendment to the Constitution ensured that, "Americans give religious liberty through the First Amendment to the Constitution," which reads: "Congress shall make no law respecting an establishment of religion or prohibiting the free exercise thereof."

Religious liberty opened the door to the great diversity of American religious life, a sectarian pluralism previously unknown in the world. Yet from the colonial period to the twenty-first century, Americans granted religious liberty grudgingly. Each new communion faces the possibility of a long haul to make its case in the American public square where opinion and even punitive action often transpire. Even a brief list illustrates the pluralism of faith and social harassment:

- Colonial Baptists exiled from Massachusetts; jailed as nonconformists; churches sometimes boarded up, 1640s.
- Colonial Quakers exiled to the Caribbean; Mary Dyer, Quaker preacher, executed in Boston, for preaching Quaker views, 1660.
- Shaker Founder Mother Ann Lee, preaching in Massachusetts, attacked by mobs, severely weakened, died in 1784.
- Joseph Smith, Mormon Founder, mayor of Nauvoo, Illinois, shot by an anti-Mormon mob while jailed in Carthage, Illinois, June 27, 1844.
- Bloody Monday, August 6, 1855, Louisville, Kentucky, Anti-Catholic mobs attack German and Italian immigrants to keep them from voting, Catholic churches ransacked; twenty-two killed.
- *Minersville School District v. Gobitis*, 1940, Supreme Court ruled that public schools could compel Jehovah's Witness-oriented students to say the pledge of allegiance to the U.S. flag. Numerous children expelled from schools throughout the country.

- KKK bombing of the Sixteenth Street Baptist Church, Birmingham, Alabama, September 15, 1963, resulted in the deaths of four elementary school age girls in a Sunday school class.
- Sikh Temple, Oak Creek, Wisconsin, six people killed by white supremacist, August 5, 2012.
- June 17, 2015, Emanuel African Methodist Episcopal Church, Charleston, South Carolina, nine people shot to death by a white supremacist.
- Churches, synagogues, mosques burned or vandalized across multiple generations throughout the United States.

## Dissent Inside and Outside the Church: Taking a Chance on Grace

Such a list brings us back to Muhammad Ali. In one of multiple interviews rebroadcast after his death, Ali recounted his own struggles over race and religion. Growing up Baptist, he continually asked his mother: "Why is Jesus white?" noting that in all the pictures of Jesus, Mary, and the angels, "everybody is white." He then recalled his return to Louisville after winning a gold medal in the 1968 Olympics, going to a local restaurant and ordering two hot dogs. "We don't serve Negroes," the waitress told him. "That's okay," Ali replied. "I don't eat them either. Bring me two hot dogs." They threw him out. "It was my home town," he said, "where I went to church." So the incongruity of segregation and "Christian America" led him to Black Muslim leader Elijah Muhammad, and from there to Islam. The interview ends with Ali's reflection on boxing and, by implication, religion: "Faith is taking a chance that you may lose."

When cynicism overwhelms, I'll try to remember the night in a Louisville cathedral when Muhammad Ali kissed me on the cheek, when an interfaith congregation reached out in thanksgiving, and when, for one brief, shining moment, God's New Day came near. Sometimes grace really does lead us home.[23]

# 7

# Life in the Spirit: Monks, Mystics, and Meditation

*"If we want to have a spiritual life, we will have to concentrate on doing so. Spirituality does not come by breathing."*[1]

Joan Chittister

The church was full of birds, at least it was when I was there. In January of 2006 for about a week, I went to mass at 5:00 every morning in the Catholic church across the street from the Mekong River in Ben Tre, Vietnam. I was there with a group of Wake Forest University students participating in a service project deep in the jungle. But we stayed in Ben Tre, the provincial capital, in a hotel next door to the Catholic church. And every morning at 5:00 they rang the bells, like a kind of Jesus fire alarm sounding across the darkness of the river and the town. And, by God (I'm speaking theologically here) people showed up, sandal-shod, tripping in sleepily to receive the body and blood of Jesus Christ while the roosters crowed in the courtyard. Men sat on one side of the church, women on the other, and before mass began they chanted the rosary antiphonally in a sanctuary filled with birds (sparrows, mostly), also singing at the top of their lungs. The birds apparently made their home under the eaves of the roof and since the windows were wide open they seemed quite happy to join the liturgy. The birds were literally in the belfry and everywhere else in the sanctuary.

So for six mornings of my life, in the predawn light of the Mekong, I think I heard Jesus in the chants of Catholics and the chirps of sparrows, neither of whose languages I could understand. It was one of the most memorable spiritual experiences of my life. Whatever the word *spirituality* means, it surely involves moments of unexpected grace within, without, and beyond our temporal, mortal selves.

For the church, the language of the Spirit and the pursuit of the spiritual life was there from the beginning. Matthew's Gospel says: "Then Jesus was led up by the Spirit into the wilderness to be tempted by the devil" (Matthew 4:1). An entire Gospel later, Mark says that, "They went to a place called Gethsemane, and he said to his disciples, 'Sit here while I pray'" (Mark 14:32). Paul told the Corinthians that, "I know a person in Christ who fourteen years ago was caught up to the third heaven—whether in the body or out of the body I do not know." He even added that the encounter involved "things that are not to be told, that no other mortal is permitted to repeat"

(2 Corinthians 12:2, 4). The actual origins of the church are often traced to events on the day of Pentecost when, "suddenly from heaven there came a sound like the rush of a violent wind, and it filled the entire house where they were sitting. . . . All of them were filled with the Holy Spirit and began to speak in other languages . . ." (Acts 2:2, 4). Three thousand converts from all over—Medes, Persians, et al.—were made that day, and the church was underway. Whether in the wilderness, the garden, the "third heaven," or a barricaded upper room, the life of the Spirit is an integral part of Christian history that no *guide* can overlook.

## Spirituality: A Moveable Feast

From the New Testament era forward, Christian individuals and communities have pursued the deeper life of spirituality, which carried them beyond "corpse-cold creedalism," or simply "getting saved," or securing a one-stop Jesus vaccination that settles things for eternity. Rather, they sought to continually cultivate the practice of the presence of God in their own daily lives, being *in*, but not *of*, the world.

Approaches to the spiritual life varied considerably, of course. Some, like St. Anthony, sought spiritual encounter in hermit-like solitude on the edges of society. Others, like St. Benedict of Nursia, found spiritual fulfillment in the communal monastic life, within the daily rhythms of work and worship, prayer and obedience. Protestants such as Philip Jacob Spener, August Herman Franke, and John Wesley himself, moved through varying dogmas—Lutheran, Calvinist, Arminian—to the pietism of heart religion, nurtured in small groups for prayer and devotional Bible study, *ecclesiolae in ecclesia*, little churches within the church. Some, like the medieval St. Teresa of Avila and the modern Howard Thurman, sought or were overtaken by mystical encounter with God, known in moments of "union" with the Transcendent One.

Still others, like the American Shakers, believed that their apocalyptic society was the avant-garde of Christ's kingdom, where there was neither "marrying nor giving in marriage" (normative celibacy), where all were equal, and where "the gift to be simple" was the gift to be spiritually free. Even amid twenty-first-century secular societies, the quest for spirituality is not lost on many so-called "nones," who, although claiming no formal religious affiliation, described themselves as "spiritual but not religious," or "believers but not belongers," building their own spirituality from a variety of sources.

## Spirituality: What in the (Other) World Is It?

Defining spirituality is no easy matter since it exists in so many forms in so many different religious traditions. In his introduction to the topic, philosopher Roger Gottlieb lists the common features of "spiritual illumination," including "acceptance of reality rather than resistance to it"; "gratitude" rather than greed; compassionately connecting to others instead of "isolation"; "and a profound, joyous, nongrasping enjoyment of life." Also, even amid the great diversity of options for exploring spirituality, the pursuit helps us discover "who we are," warts and all, and an ability to experience "the miraculous nature of the ordinary."[2]

In her study of the *Rule of St. Benedict*, Benedictine Joan Chittister writes that one element of spirituality involves an awareness "of what is going on around us and allowing ourselves to feel its effects." A second element encompasses "learning to hear what God wants in any given situation" and a willingness to respond to it. She concludes that, recognizing greed or violence in the world but failing to ask "what the Gospel expects in such a situation is not spirituality."[3]

---

That is a beautiful description.

**THE ACOLYTE**

---

In her study of *Christian Spirituality*, British historian Karen Smith insists that for the church, spirituality requires continuing dialogue between "doctrine and experience." Yet she also suggests that "a sense of longing or desire is at the root of every expression of Christian spirituality." This often-intangible element is bound up in "a search for meaning" within the context of the Jesus Story.[4]

So Christian spirituality is essentially a quest for continuing encounter with the God revealed in Jesus Christ. It involves not simply conversion as a one-time salvific event, but as an entry point to a life of spiritual pursuit. Whether in solitude, community, or direct engagement in and with the world, practitioners throughout church history attest to the practice of the Presence in ecstatic experiences, and in encounters of the Spirit amid the pain, suffering, injustice, and poverty of those in greatest need. Given the diversity of definitions and approaches to Christian spirituality in the church's history, this chapter provides illustrations through specific examples, including monastic communitarianism, Pietism, mysticism, and Pentecostalism.

## Spiritual Formation: Meeting the Shakers

In October of 1974, my friend Bud Williams and I drove from our homes in Southborough, Massachusetts to the Shaker settlement at Canterbury, New Hampshire. Bud was a deacon in the First Community Church of Southborough, where I was the pastor. At Canterbury we met the last three Shaker sisters living in that Protestant, monastic-like community established in 1792 as part of the group's initial fervor in colonial America. From the late eighteenth to the early twentieth centuries, the United Society of Believers in Christ's Second Appearing (the Shakers' formal name) in Canterbury and a dozen or so other communities thrived numerically and financially through community farming, woodworking, and inventions such as the flat-sided broom and the clothespin (honest!). They also took in runaway slaves and offered shelter to orphans and abused women and children. But by the time Bud Williams and I arrived, Canterbury village was down to its last members, the three sisters—Gertrude Soule, Miriam Wall, and Bertha Lindsay—who were in their seventies and eighties.

Bud and I were the only visitors that day, and the women, clad in long dresses and prayer caps, invited us into their living room for tea and conversation. If memory serves, each of them had grown up in the community, entering as children and committing themselves to the

Shaker life when they reached adulthood. They had a few books for sale, and I purchased one that I have to this day. The three Shaker sisters signed the book, and one of them remarked: "When we are dead this will be worth some money!" Bud Williams, never given to subtlety, asked outright: "What will happen when you are all gone?" Eldress Gertrude Soule gave a brief but eloquent response that I later heard her repeat in various articles and documentaries: "We may die out, but the Spirit will reveal itself again, somewhere, somehow, if people want to live a Kingdom life." That visit, and Eldress Gertrude's insight, remains one of the most memorable experiences of my own spiritual pursuits.

---

That will preach. Some spiritually confident people are just annoying. Others are confident on behalf of God—that confidence is contagious.

THE DEACON

---

Just when we were feeling all spiritual, Bud Williams had another question. Noting a portable television complete with antenna in the corner of the living room, Williams asked with some dismay: "So do you ladies watch television?" To which one of the sainted sisters replied: "O yes, we wouldn't miss the hockey games!" Apparently, worldliness can find its way into the most spiritual environs and individuals. Perhaps it was always thus.

## Martyrdom of the Spirit: The Monastic Revolution

The Shakers were, in effect, a Protestant monastic community, born of the visions, voices, and revelations of their founder, Mother Ann Lee. Such monastic enthusiasm and formation was certainly not new in Christian history. When the Constantinian era brought relative peace to the church, and the martyrs' fires turned to ash, it wasn't long before some people worried that the heart had gone out of Christian spirituality. As social privilege became ecclesiastically acceptable, a number of spiritually hardy folks looked for another kind of martyrdom, that of the spirit. As "red martyrdom"—sacrificing one's life for the faith—diminished, some spoke of "white martyrdom," surrendering to a life of self-sacrifice and intense practice of the presence of God.

These individuals chose to surrender themselves by relinquishing the world, the flesh, and the devil, distancing themselves (literally and figuratively) from society's corrupting environs; and cultivating an ascetic life of self-denial regarding personal possessions, food, clothing, social status, and yes, even sex (especially sex). Their energies and efforts involved the nurture of a life of meditation and prayer, particularly intercessory prayer, as well as the study and contemplation of holy writ. Some chose to create spiritual enclaves in the city, looking temptation in the face as a witness against urban degeneracy. Others sought solitude in the wilderness, removed from the distractions and protection of this present evil age—meeting the Tempter, as Jesus did in the desert.

But whatever their locale, in solitude or community, these pilgrims of the Spirit gave witness to the demands of the gospel and the power of intercessory prayer and practice, in the world but not of it. This martyrdom of the spirit was at the heart of the monastic revolution, born of sacrifice, discipline, and a radical declaration that the prayers of the monks hold the world together, whether the people in the world knew it or not. So from the third-century desert fathers and mothers, to the United Society of Believers in Christ's Second Appearing in Canterbury, New Hampshire, the church has long known those who sought to live a "kingdom life" as a witness of the world to come in the world as it is.

## Christian Monasticism: A School of Christ's Service

Monasticism took shape by the late third century, personified in the life of Anthony, whose spiritual exploits in the desert of North Africa are documented in the fourth-century biography written by the prominent bishop, Athanasius of Alexandria. Anthony lived to be 105, surviving for years on a diet of water, bread, and salt. He fought the forces of darkness including wild beasts, evil spirits, and even the specter of females, a vision of whom brought the temptations of the flesh, all of which Anthony resisted. He lived alone as a hermit, a spiritual lifestyle that became known as anchoritic monastic life, a solitary existence outside civilization and community.

---

My doctor told me I had too much bread and salt in my diet. Maybe someone should make a St. Anthony diet book.

THE ELDER

---

As a youth reared in a Christian environment, Anthony was captivated by a text that would challenge persons throughout monastic history, as Jesus says to the so-called rich young ruler, "If you would be perfect, go, sell all you have and give to the poor, and come, follow me" (Matthew 19:21). That same verse, some 800 years later, would seize a young Francis of Assisi (1209) in the depth of his being, sending him into the streets and highways to live and work with lepers and the poor. The emphasis on "perfection" was essentially sanctification or deification, giving oneself to the cultivation of the spiritual life in order to experience Christ's presence, conform to his image, and cultivate the gifts of the Spirit.

Anthony's reputation for holy living brought other individuals who drew near to him as he modeled the life of the Spirit. These were perhaps the first monastic communities, with hermits continuing to live separately, but in close proximity. By the time of Anthony's death in 356, communities of monks and hermits had sprung up across North Africa, constructing ways of living, worshiping, and praying together.

Anchorite (hermit) existence could get weird, however, as represented in a group known as Stylites, individuals who chose to live on the top of columns constructed in the desert, or Dendrites, who spent their time in trees. Simeon the Stylite (d. 458) is perhaps the best known, dwelling some thirty-seven years on a pillar near Antioch. His spirituality was so respected that pilgrims came from far and wide to secure his advice and his prayers.[5] Truly, Simeon was a living martyr!

Pachomius (d. 346) was another important North African monastic founder and father figure who developed a specific rule for communal holy living and holy dying, founding some eleven monasteries (nine for men; two for women). Monks relinquished worldly goods, took solemn vows to God and the order, and cultivated a life of work and prayer. Those considering monastic life were required to complete at least a yearlong novitiate, experiencing communal disciplines before taking solemn vows.[6]

## Monastic Worship: The *opus Dei*

Cenobitic monasticism—that is, life in community—ultimately became a more normative option than the hermit life as monastic communities sprang up in the church, East and West. These gatherings were often formed around a "rule" that governed behavior and provided a sense of identity in specific monastic orders. For example, the Order of St. Benedict was established in Subiaco, Italy, in 529, and centered in the *opus Dei*, the Divine work, that informed the entirety of monastic communal life. Observing the canonical hours, the community gathered throughout the day, beginning in the wee hours of the morning for vigils, a time of fighting the principalities and powers when the rest of the world was fast asleep and spiritually vulnerable.

Prayer, Benedict believed, was best when brief, focused, and continuous. Thus the monastic day was divided into seven brief periods for prayer, particularly the utilization of the Psalms, chanting through all 150 in a calendar year. The times included Lauds, Prime, Terce, Sext, None, Vespers, and Compline. Vigils were added in predawn darkness. Thus Benedict concluded that while God's presence was everywhere in the world, "beyond the least doubt we should believe this to be especially true when we celebrate the Divine Office."[7]

## Monastic Vows

Monks take vows. They pledge themselves to God and community as a framework for the Spirit. Benedictines illustrate the point with their threefold vows of obedience, stability, and something called *conversatio morum.*

- **Obedience** means relinquishing one's own will in order to "listen" appropriately and insightfully to other sources, including God, Scripture, the *Rule*, and of course the Abbot, who represents Christ in the community. The Prologue to Benedict's *Rule* instructs the monk, "This message of mine is for you, then, if you are ready to give up your own will, once and for all, and armed with the strong and noble weapons of obedience to do battle for Jesus, the Christ."[8]
- **Stability** requires the monk to make a commitment to a particular place, the specific monastic community where the individual has chosen to pursue the spiritual life. This vow marks one's willingness, not simply to become a Benedictine, but to live that life in an explicit location with others who have identified with that location and its particular history. This reflects an important

reality of spirituality, monastic or not: Sometimes, when we cannot believe for ourselves, the community—monastic, congregational, communal—believes *for* us. The Benedictine vow of stability makes that reality tangible in an identifiable community and actual place.

- ***Conversatio Morum*** involves a commitment toward "conversion to a monastic way of life" that incorporates poverty (relinquishing material goods), chastity (a celibate life), silence (a willingness to listen outside oneself), and a conformity to the communal life of worship, prayer, and shared labor.[9]

## Monasteries: A Prophetic Witness

Monastic communities offered prophetic witness to the church that in many ways reshaped the nature of the church itself. First, they provided an environment for the promotion and cultivation of the spiritual life. Perhaps it was less that monastic communities of males or females escaped the world than that they offered an alternative world for seeking God. Students often ask why monks did not engage the society as Jesus instructed his followers to do. The fact is, the monks did confront the world through the witness of their common life of prayer and intercession. And many were not completely cloistered, educating the young, or carrying for the sick, the poor, and the marginalized. Through it all, there was the ministry of intercession, invoking God's care and protection for the world. They were a school of the Lord's service; that was their witness in the world.

THE BISHOP

> I think we need to create new forms of prophetic alternative communities that work in and with the church. Too often Protestants create these communities by exiting their homes rather than staying within them.

Second, the earliest monasteries were a reassertion of the laity as a spiritual resource in the face of a hierarchical, clergy-dominated church. The earliest communities were composed largely of laypersons, with only a few ordained individuals to provide pastoral care and consecrate the sacraments. Women's orders received the sacraments from priests who served as confessors. Third, the communal nature of monastic life reminded the church of the dangers of materialism and the distractions of possessions and wealth. From Pachomius, one of the great fourth-century founders of monasticism, to Francis of Assisi in the thirteenth century, the words of Jesus to the "rich young ruler" were galvanizing: "If any want to become my followers, let them deny themselves and take up their cross and follow me" (Matthew 16:24). Others discovered monastic spirituality in Jesus's commission to his disciples and other followers as described in Matthew 10 and Luke 10, sending them out in great vulnerability without "purse, cloak, staff, or shoes." The community of goods that is at the heart of monastic life was born of the earliest description of the post-Pentecost Christians who "shared all things in common."

Fourth, monastic celibacy was itself an ultimate form of self-sacrifice, and a decision to engage in the monastic family of communal living. Finally, monasteries systematized the daily liturgical experiences that facilitated monastic intention to work, to worship, and to pray. That tradition continues into the twenty-first century but not without significant numerical declines in monastic communities, particularly in the West. As one monk told me, "In America and Europe, everyone wants to take a retreat at a monastery, but no one wants to become a monk!"

## Mysticism: Finding Union with the Divine (and Being a Little Weird)

The monastic environment was a seedbed of Christian mysticism. Mystics flourished throughout the life of the church, but monasteries were particularly favorable settings for mystical exploration. When I've required students to read some of the best-known mystics of the Christian church—Julian of Norwich, Francis of Assisi, Margaret Kempe, Teresa of Avila, John of the Cross—some of the students will inevitably say something like: "This person really knew how to struggle with and experience the presence of God. But he/she's really weird, maybe even a little crazy." Mystics *are* a little weird, or at least given to eccentricity, even as they reflect some of the church's most profound and colorful forms of spirituality. The traditional "mystic way"—awakening, purification, union—with a "dark night of the soul" thrown in for good measure, serves as a guide for experiences that are themselves unpredictable and expansive.

THE ELDER

I like to think of myself as a second-hand mystic. I love reading mystics, reading about mystics, and imagining what would happen if I were a real one. I am saving actual mysticism for retirement.

In his classic work, *The Varieties of Religious Experience* (1902), William James identifies four elements for understanding mystic spirituality:

- *Ineffability*: It is beyond words; all descriptions or explanations are inadequate to describe the depth of the mystical experience.
- *Noetic Quality*: Mystical encounters "are states of insight into depths of truth unplumbed by the discursive intellect." In other words, they offer new illuminations and revelations that are full of significance and importance, beyond the normal rational or intellectual categories or methods of investigation. As such they bear "a curious sense of authority" that remains when the mystical event has passed.[10]

- *Transiency*: "Mystical states cannot be sustained for long." James even suggests specific time frames of half an hour, two hours maximum. Human beings cannot sustain that kind of intense mystical ecstasy. They need not, but may, recur, however.[11]
- *Passivity*: While individuals may pursue certain historic or traditional steps toward mystical engagement with the Divine, once it is secured, mystics often feel as if their own will is "in abeyance," and they are "grasped and held by a superior power."[12]

While James's description of mysticism is not limited to Christianity, it is a valuable tool for understanding the nature of mystical experience in the history of the church. Since this book is merely a *guide* to Christian history, perhaps one way to illustrate the nature of Christian mysticism, particularly as outlined by William James, is to reflect on two examples of the mystical life in two different eras of history. They are Teresa of Avila the medieval Spanish saint and clairvoyant, and Howard Thurman, the twentieth-century African American mystic, writer, and preacher.

## Teresa of Avila: Mysticism in Action

The Spanish Carmelite, Teresa of Avila (1515–1582), is one of the church's best-known and most widely read mystics. Her experiences and approach to the mystical life are documented in her autobiography and in other works such as *The Interior Castle* and *The Way of Perfection*. Joining a Carmelite order based in the Spanish mountain town of Avila, Teresa struggled for years with her own sinfulness and searched for a deepening encounter with the Divine. Ultimately she experienced a conversion brought on by a recognition of the sacrifice of Christ as exemplified in a statue known as *Ecce Homo*, "behold the man," a bust depicting his head crowned with thorns and his face marked with blood.

In one of the most famous passages of her autobiography, Teresa describes a continuing mystical vision in which she would sometimes encounter "an angel in bodily form" who "was not tall, but short, and very beautiful," his face all "aflame."[13] It gets better. The angel has a long spear with which "he seemed to pierce my heart several times so that it penetrated my entrails," with a pain "so sharp it made me utter several moans" with a "sweetness" so intense "that one can never wish to lose it, nor will one's soul be content with anything less than God."[14] In this fascinating passage, the links between flesh and spirit, sexuality and spirituality, pain and ecstasy, are united in a direct encounter of the soul with God.

Teresa reports a wide variety of visions, many of which include conversations with "Our Lady" (the Virgin Mary), and with Jesus himself, who on one occasion "talked" with her and "reminded me of how wicked my life had been and made me feel very confused and distressed." Mystical experiences could bring great joy but also demand repentance and a sense of sinfulness.[15]

In *Varieties of Religious Experience*, William James devotes considerable attention to Teresa of Avila as an extraordinary representative of the broader mystic-tradition of Christianity, particularly Roman Catholicism, noting that "the deliciousness of some of these [mystical] states seems to be beyond anything known in ordinary consciousness." Some of the mystical encounters are indeed beyond words, and beyond rational comprehension, a sense of "*raptus* or ravishment" that at times seems to separate soul and body in a living human being. Indeed, he urges reading Teresa's mystical accounts with the consideration that "one is dealing, not with imaginary experiences, but with phenomena which, however rare, follow perfectly definite psychological types."[16]

---

How does one know if they've had a mystical encounter? I mean, we can read about them but their reality isn't transferable like geometry theorems.

THE ACOLYTE

---

Teresa's mystical experience impelled her to action. In 1562, to considerable controversy, she founded in Avila the Convent of the Discalced (barefoot) Carmelites, a highly cloistered order given to contemplation and intercessory prayer. In this endeavor she was assisted by another of the great Spanish mystics, John of the Cross, who established a male monastic community of Discalced Carmelites in 1568, also with extensive persecution from the Spanish Catholic establishment. Teresa was canonized in 1622. In 1970, Pope Paul VI bestowed on her the highly exalted title of Doctor of the Church, a title reserved for only the most prominent of the saints who offer lasting contributions to the Catholic theology, inspiration, and identity.

## Howard Thurman: Mysticism and Social Action

Some five centuries after Teresa of Avila explored the "interior castle," Howard Thurman (1899–1981), African American teacher, preacher, and writer, reflected a mystical approach to faith and life distinct from, but no less powerful than, that of the Spanish Catholic. Born in Florida in 1899, Thurman was reared primarily by his grandmother who nurtured his religious experience and his desire for education. He graduated from Morehouse College in 1923, the same year he was admitted to Rochester Theological Seminary, a German Baptist-founded school that allowed for admission of only two African American students a year.[17]

After graduation, Thurman read *Finding the Trail of Life*, one of Rufus Jones's many works on Christian spirituality, and he determined to find a way to study with "this wonderful philosopher-mystic."[18] Thus Thurman wound up in what he called "independent study" with the Quaker professor at Haverford College. Jones, one of the early twentieth century's widely recognized mystics and student of mysticism, found resources for Thurman to pursue their studies together, outside the segregationist admission policies of the college. Jones was among those individuals who insisted that all persons had the ability to experience mystical encounters, and many of his writings were aimed at awakening that realization in the public square.[19]

Jones acknowledged that mystics did indeed reflect "psychical abnormality . . . doubtful metaphysical theory," and an excess of "gullibility." But he affirmed that those persons also reflected "an irresistible consciousness of contact with God."[20]

Rufus Jones is best described as a "practical mystic," who defined "vital inward religion" as "an actual personal contact with the central eternal Stream of Life." Yet he also insisted that "it is an historically untenable position" to suggest "that an inner religious experience" could be separated from direct engagement in society, particularly efforts to make "the area of the Kingdom of God wider" in the world.[21] That linkage between the "inner and outer life" clearly contributed to Thurman's own sense of spirituality and social engagement.

Rochester Seminary gave great emphasis to the Social Gospel, due in large part to the continuing influence of Social Gospel leader Walter Rauschenbusch who taught there for many years. Thurman was captivated by Social Gospel imperatives, and it was evident in his first, and perhaps best-known, book, *Jesus and the Disinherited* (1949). Thurman moved through multiple institutions as local church pastor, dean of the chapels at Howard and Boston Universities, and founder of the Church for the Fellowship of all Peoples, a congregation that anticipated later emphases on religious pluralism, racial and class diversity, and spiritual renewal.

---

*Jesus and the Disinherited* changed my life. Not reading it is a very poor life decision.

**THE DEACON**

---

Howard Thurman's own direct encounters with the Divine began in his youth, one in 1910 when he observed the return of Haley's Comet. Terrified, he sought solace from his grandmother, who responded, "Nothing will happen to us, Howard. God will take care of us." Thurman concluded that right then, "something was touched and kindled in me, a quiet reassurance that has never quite deserted me. . . . It was this inarticulate awareness that silenced my fear and stilled my panic."[22] Reflecting on that event as an adult, Thurman insisted that it began in him the recognition of "the 'givenness of God' as expressed in the hunger of the heart," an early sense of mystical quest.[23] Mystical experiences could come at any time, when sought or when interpreted by others.

This encounter was the center of human life; better yet, for Thurman, it *centered* human life. He wrote that when the hunger of the human heart "merges with what seems to be the fundamental intent of life, [then] communion with God the Creator of Life is not only possible but urgent."[24] But this "communion with God" was inseparable from issues of justice in the church and the larger human society. At every turn, Howard Thurman did not hesitate to address the Social Gospel and its implications for church and world. Addressing the importance of racial justice and reconciliation, Thurman wrote decisively: "The walls [of racism] that divide must be abolished. They must be cast down, destroyed, uprooted. This is beyond debate." Racial "barriers" should be recognized for what they really meant: "a disease of our society, the enemy of human decency and human respect."[25] Thus, in American society of the mid-twentieth century, "the burden of being black and the burden of being white is so heavy that it is rare in our society to experience oneself as a human being." Rather, the experience of being human required "experiencing one's fellows as human beings."[26] Faith, Thurman insisted, teaches us that God *is*; that God is *near*; and that God is love.[27] That simple confession may well have summed up Howard Thurman's mystical and activist vision toward a beloved community.

## Mysticism: A Spiritual Democracy

Thurman's mystic-mentor, Rufus Jones, insisted that mystical encounter, what he called "the experience of direct communication of the soul with God," was available to every human being.[28] It was not limited to an esoteric, eccentric spiritual elect. Rather, Jones was convinced of "an unfathomable depth of inward Godlike Being" at the "spiritual centre" of every human person. This spiritual center could become "a transmissive medium of the highest significance," or "buried deep under the piles of rubbish which merely secular pursuits . . . may accumulate."[29] Jones proposed a vision of a people's mysticism, in which spiritual encounter was available to those who cultivated the Divine presence. St. Teresa and "St. Howard" illustrate two diverse paths to such mystical encounter, a trail of pilgrims undiminished in the church's history.

## Twenty-First Century Spirituality: Cut, Paste, and Meditate

Those interested in investigating the presence and pluralism of "spirituality" in heartland American culture needed only to attend (as I did) the Bele Chere weekend in Asheville, North Carolina. The annual street festival attracts tourists, musicians, artists, and religionists galore to that

Appalachian town, just off the Blue Ridge Parkway. The signs of popular spirituality were evident on every corner. Methodists sold bottled water and soft drinks, while Baptists offered gospel tracts as a witness for Christ. (The message of the tracts cut to the chase: "Turn or Burn!") Hare Krishna devotees with shaven heads and saffron robes distributed copies of the *Bhagavad Gita*, proffering their own witness to the presence of god(s) in the world(s). NASCAR drivers (representing one of America's most powerful religions) let people ride around in their cars. One row of shops boasted storefront centers housing such diverse religious groups as the Islamic Society and the ECKANKAR meditation movement. The lobby of a health-food restaurant posted brochures for Psychic Tarot Readings, whose "psychic-sensitive" medium was "an apprentice of renowned Native American medicine man and author, Sun Bear." If tarot readers, Muslims, and Hindus are in Asheville, North Carolina, that Baptist-infested mountain town, then they are everywhere! Spirituality in its diverse forms is finding its way into regions that once were dominated by church steeples, tent revivals, and the King James Version of the Bible. While polls suggest the rise of the "nones," those who claim no involvement in organized religions, many of those same people consider themselves "spiritual but not religious," in their pursuits of inner-related wholeness and contemplation.

Certainly, preoccupation with spirituality is nothing new. Religious awakenings and enthusiasms, traditional and nontraditional, seem endemic to the inner life of Christians in every era. The end of the nineteenth century evidenced significant public pursuit of what today might be called "holistic religion," manifested in Christian Science,

---

I took a survey in my diocese and half chose the label "none." Since then I have wondered if the phenomenon is more a result of the explosion of spiritual and religious options beyond the orthodox labels rather than validation of the secularization thesis.

**THE BISHOP**

---

Spiritualism, Homeopathy, Seventh Day Adventism, and meditation practices influenced by Eastern religions. The World's Parliament of Religions, held in Chicago in 1893, included representatives of the great world faith communions in an effort to survey the changing spiritual environment of the then modern world.

Few observers of twenty-first-century culture would deny that there is an increasing curiosity about, if not participation in, varying dimensions of the spiritual life. In its broadest sense, this concern for spirituality involves ways of practicing the presence of God, the Sacred, or the Other, through innumerable, sometimes highly symbolic, means. These methods, drawn from a variety of sources, ancient and modern, illustrate important re-formations in the religious terrain. Thus, while interest in spirituality is certainly not new, contemporary persons are exploring an ever-increasing number of paths to the spiritual life manifested inside and outside traditional religious institutions. In short, large numbers of persons, particularly in the

West, seem concerned about spiritual fulfillment and, like good western consumers, are willing to shop around until they find what they are looking for. In the quest for spiritual experience, the lines between Catholic and Protestant, liturgical and nonliturgical, Christian and non-Christian practices are becoming increasingly blurred. In a sense, one element of newness in the current phenomenon is the way in which seekers blend multiple religious traditions, methodologies, and literature in their search for the spiritual. Inside and outside the Christian church, the pursuit of spirituality may involve some or all of the following:

- Use of diverse sources from spiritual literature as guides to meditation, contemplation, or inner reflection. These include certain "classics of Christian devotion" that may include writers from the early Christian centuries, varying mystical treatises—Teresa's *Interior Castle*; *The Living Flame of Love* (St. John of the Cross); Blaise Pascal's *Pensées*; as well as more contemporary spiritual writings by C. S. Lewis, Thomas Merton, Dorothy Day, Dietrich Bonhoeffer, Frederick Buechner, Desmond Tutu, Parker Palmer, Kathleen Norris, and Henri Nouwen (to name only a few).
- Many seekers have secured the services of *spiritual friends*, or *spiritual guides*, to shape their spiritual formation in particular ways. These guides often provide meditative techniques, help negotiate spiritual struggles, and offer a source of interpretation to readings and reflections.
- Churches have begun to expand traditional programs or develop new ones for nurturing

spirituality for those so interested in prayer groups, devotional bible study, "pub theology" gatherings, and other small-group meditation experiences.

- Many Christians (and non-Christians) have moved to incorporate broader readings and meditative techniques from other religions than their own. I know a Buddhist abbot who partners with a Catholic priest to lead groups using Christian/Buddhist practices. The Vietnamese Buddhist Thich Nhat Hanh, author of the best-seller *Living Buddha, Living Christ*, has become a spiritual guide for many seekers drawing on both traditions. He writes: "To me, [Buddhist] mindfulness is very much like the Holy spirit. Both are agents of healing. . . . The Buddha was called the King of Healers. In the Bible, when someone touches Christ, he or she is healed."[30]
- Many twenty-first-century Christians are extending their ritual participation into other religions, seeking the meditative powers of Native American sweat-lodges, Jewish Seders, Buddhist temples, and Hindu ashrams. Sometimes they have been welcomed; at other times the devotees of the other religions have questioned whether Christians should be "experimenting" with their traditions when they do not intend to stay.
- The widely renewed concern for spiritual form has also encouraged many to go on pilgrimage, an ancient tradition characteristic of many religious groups. Christians the world over make pilgrimages to holy sites from Rome to Alexandria, Jerusalem to Lourdes, or the shrine of Our Lady of

> Guadalupe. Some have chosen to walk the *camino* to Santiago de Compostela in Spain, or the Appalachian Trail in the U.S. As Richard R. Niebuhr writes: "Pilgrims are persons in motion—passing through territories not their own—seeking something we might call completion, or perhaps the word clarity will do as well, a goal to which only the spirit's compass points the way."[31]

Niebuhr's comment that pilgrims pass "through territories not their own" speaks of a kind of spiritual wistfulness, a yearning, a longing search for experiences, however transient or momentary, that carry us beyond ourselves, outside the religious or ideological status quo. Such wistful occurrences are seldom calculated, but find us when we least expect.

In Vietnam, a territory definitely not my own, I learned those wistful lessons again. On that 2006 trip I joined two faculty colleagues and twelve Wake Forest undergraduates in helping build a two-room school in a Mekong Delta commune so far back in the sticks that the teachers had to pick us up on motorbikes to carry us the last few miles, as deep inside any "wilderness" as I had ever been before. For days we worked with the locals painting, planting, and otherwise preparing the building for a new generation of Vietnamese students. Our hosts, a married couple who were civic officials in the commune, prepared lunch for us daily, and stretched hammocks for afternoon naps around their spacious dirt-floored, thatch-roofed house. On one wall there were old photos of the couple in their youth, holding rifles and dressed in the pajama-like uniforms of the Viet Cong. They were both combatants in what the Vietnamese call the "American War."

When the work ended and the school dedicated, our Wake Forest group departed amid hugs and tears from a brief but astonishingly profound experience. A year later, one of our colleagues returned to the commune and discovered that while the school was still intact, much of the village had been washed away in a devastating typhoon. The house where we took meals and naps was gone, with only the wooden beams and doorposts remaining.

She also discovered that after our departure, our hosts, the former Viet Cong, had carved each of our names on the beam at the entrance to what had been and would be again their home. So for one brief, wistful moment, a group of all-too-privileged Americans understood something of the unexpected grace of community, perhaps even spirituality, carved quite literally on a doorpost in a Mekong Delta commune.

Will such halting, albeit singularly overpowering, moments eradicate decades of geopolitical, ideological conflict in Viet Nam, Iraq, Afghanistan, Libya, Israel/Palestine, or Washington, D.C.? Of course not. Two-room schoolhouses and names on Viet Cong doorposts won't transform complex global struggles anytime soon. The "rough places," as the prophet Isaiah calls them, are still as rough as can be. But still we cling to wistfulness—that mixture of sadness, expectation, and yearning for something beyond ourselves, a determination that, against all odds, we can work for transformation on this earth.

8

# In the World but (Mostly) Not of It: Modernity and Gospel

*"The Modernist is deliberately undertaking to adjust Christianity to modern needs by changing the emphasis in its message and by historically evaluating and restating the permanent significance of evangelical Christianity to human life."*
Shailer Mathews, *The Faith of Modernism*, 1924

*"Judged by its fruits, new theology, another name for Modernism, has no defense for its existence; while conservatism has given to the world its Christianity, and to Christ His Church."*
W. B. Riley, *The Menace of Modernism*, 1917

## Modernity and the New Morality: A Painful Memoir

"Modernity," at least certain religious implications of it, descended on me at a student retreat at the Broadway Baptist Church in Fort Worth, Texas, in the year of our Lord, 1965. I was a college fresh-person, and the retreat centered on certain moral imperatives, situation ethics, and the so-called New Morality that marked 1960s cultural transitions.

The retreat speaker was Dr. J. P. Allen, pastor of the Broadway Church. He discussed resulting moral dilemmas, sex, dating, sex, Christian values, sex, human relationships and, you know, sex. When he finished, Dr. Allen asked for questions and I bounded to my feet, full of relentless adolescent and evangelical zeal, both of which can kill you. "Well," I opined, "I find that if we just trust Jesus, and walk with him daily, God will take care of all these moral issues."

THE ACOLYTE

I don't think anyone in my youth group has said such a thing.

Dr. J. P. Allen set his jaw, looked straight into my post-pubescent little eyes and responded, "Young man, everything I have said for the last hour was an attempt to avoid that kind of glib, simplistic Christianity. Try to use a little God-given reasoning, please." I cannot adequately explain it, but in the complete humiliation of that now-distant moment, I began to learn to wrestle with the inescapable dilemmas of moral, spiritual, and human life. In that wonderful/terrible encounter, I was, quite simply, born again. Without knowing it (until I told him the story years later), Dr. Allen dragged me into the Age of Reason, demanding in one brief sentence that I move beyond shallow piety to critical reflection, even in matters of faith and spirituality. Humiliation is a painful and poignant teacher that sometimes marks the beginning of real learning and real life.

---

If only Dr. Allen could drag Ken Ham into the Age of Reason.

THE DEACON

---

## Is "Modern Church" an Oxymoron?

"Modernity," a long-debated idea and construct for explaining changes in western thought and action, all with global implications, is difficult enough to define, let alone summarize. The concept is often dated from the late seventeenth and early eighteenth centuries, particularly with the rise of the Enlightenment and the application of reason to all aspects of human life. In *Modern Christianity to 1900*, Amanda Porterfield describes "modernization" as "enthusiasm for rational explanations of life that privilege individualism, nationalism, scientific enterprise, and strategic planning." She notes that while the application of modernity differed from region to region, many turned to religion for assistance in responding to social transitions evident in multiple contexts.[1] At the same time, modernity brought challenges to traditional religious dogmas and social privilege, sacramentalism, ecclesiastical authority, church economics, and the meaning of salvation itself.[2]

The breadth of modernity's impact on culture is considerable, particularly related to religion. This includes:

- A period of "discoveries." New land masses, new science, new approaches to life and faith, all challenging tradition.
- The application of science, reason, sociology, psychology, and other "new studies" to traditional ideas and institutions.
- A growing concern for and participation in various forms of technology, personally and corporately—printing, travel, public media.
- Continuing struggles/investigations of relations between reason/revelation, religious/secular cultures, pluralism/particularity.
- Impact of the Enlightenment, Romanticism, Mysticism, Modern*ism*, Fundamentalism, Individualism, and Pluralism.
- Historical-critical approaches to biblical/theological studies that divided Christians over the nature of divine revelation.
- Science as the means to "truth" educationally, morally, theologically. "All truth is God's truth" wherever it may be found.
- Rationality leads to order; order improves function. Thus scientific discoveries inevitably impact, even improve, daily life.
- The development of democratic idealism, liberationist and civil rights movements that challenged

institutionalized colonialism, racism, sexism, and other signs of oppression.

- Constructs "Grand Narratives"—culture-encompassing stories that the society uses to articulate and mythologize destiny, ideals, and actions.
- A belief that, "There is a stable, coherent, knowable self. Self is conscious, rational, autonomous."[3]

---

The number of ecclesiastical gatherings dedicated to these questions outnumber the animals on the ark.

THE BISHOP

---

I think a growing number of Christians sees these debates in the past tense.

THE ACOLYTE

---

These developments led many to believe that religious communities must come to terms with these new realities for the sake of the gospel and its relevance in the modern world. Writing from inside the church, Shailer Mathews, dean of the University of Chicago Divinity School, described *The Faith of Modernism* (1924) as "the use of the methods of modern science to find, state and use the permanent and central values of inherited orthodoxy."[4] For Mathews, these newly understood issues "cannot be quieted by mere pietism or theological dogmatism." Rather, they led to greater demands from "the masses" for women "sharing in the privileges of men," expanded educational opportunities, "adventurous" intellectualism, and the separation of religious belief from "political control." The challenge, he believed, was to maintain religion as "a vital and inspiring force" amid these new cultural, scientific, and philosophical realities.[5]

## Modernity Creates Division

Shailer Matthews was one of many religious leaders considered to be progressives, modernists, or in many cases "Christocentric liberals," individuals who were convinced that the church should come to terms with all this new knowledge. They contended that "all truth is God's truth," however it might be discovered. Church doctrine might be adapted in light of the continuing search for truth. Failure to do so could lead to the loss of future generations who would distance themselves from a faith that resisted modern insights and discoveries. Christocentric liberals were those persons who understood Christianity as open to biological evolution, utilized the historical-critical method of biblical studies, benefited from new studies in psychology and sociology, pursued philosophical exploration, particularly idealism, and promoted "moral values" within the context of modern democratic ideals.[6]

Theologically, they held a strong belief in the benevolence of God as revealed in Jesus, in the progressive evolution of human nature, and the Christian faith as grounded

Why is a scientist being faithful to his lineage by disagreeing with it, while a person of faith is disparaging theirs for the same thing?

THE ELDER

in experience with Christ. It was this experiential dimension of encounter with the Spirit of Jesus that Christocentric liberals believed to be the timeless and continuing dynamic of Christianity. Dogmas might change with time and new discoveries, but a vital experientialism with Christ endured.

Conservatives, both Catholic and Protestant, responded to these cultural and religious transitions by reasserting the timeless orthodoxy of Christian doctrine, creeds, and ethical principles. Many felt strongly that accommodation to modernity would undermine if not annihilate the faith, negotiating away the non-negotiables of a discernibly orthodox Christian tradition.

In *Christianity and Liberalism* (1923) Princeton Seminary's John Gresham Machen asserted that theological liberalism had negated Christian doctrine so dramatically that what remained "is not Christianity at all, but a religion which is so entirely different from Christianity as to belong to a distinct category."[7] Evangelist Billy Sunday said it with a characteristic bombast against liberals, shouting: "Lord, save us from off-handed, flabby-cheeked, brittle-boned, weak-kneed, thin-skinned, pliable, plastic, spineless, effeminate, ossified three-karat Christianity."[8] Enough said.

THE DEACON

Reread that Billy Sunday quote in a sweet TV preacher voice. Leave it as a voicemail for your favorite pastor. ;)

By 1910 the representatives of Protestant orthodoxy had become "Fundamentalists," because of their concern to retain and promote certain doctrinal non-negotiables (fundamentals) that included the authority of an infallible, inerrant Bible; the virgin birth of Jesus Christ, his death on the cross as a substitute for humanity's sin; his bodily resurrection from the dead; and his second coming to establish his kingdom for a thousand years (millennialism). Some added the literal miracles described in the New Testament. Fundamentalism had its roots in premillennial theology regarding Christ's return, and the Calvinistic systematic theology associated with Princeton Theological Seminary.[9]

THE ACOLYTE

Why wouldn't the fundamentals be love God and love neighbor?

## The Scopes Trial: Fundamentalists and Modernists in Tennessee

"A fundamentalist is an evangelical who is angry about something," George Marsden wrote, providing an apt description of the great orator William Jennings Bryan at the Scopes (Monkey) Trial in the summer of 1925.[10] That fascinating populist event occurred when the American Civil Liberties Union prevailed on John Scopes, biology teacher in the Dayton, Tennessee public schools, to violate the state's anti-evolution law. They hired the renowned agnostic, Clarence Darrow, to defend Scopes, while Bryan's services were offered to the prosecution. Bryan asserted that, "The parents have a right to say that no teacher paid by their money shall rob their children of faith in God and send them back to their homes skeptical, or infidels, or agnostics, or atheists."[11]

Darrow answered back: "Here, we find today as brazen and as bold an attempt to destroy learning as was ever made in the middle ages, and the only difference is we have not provided that they shall be burned at the stake, but there is time for that, your Honor."[12] What many called the "trial of the century" boiled over inside and outside Judge John Raulston's steamy courtroom, in July 1925.

Judge Raulston refused to allow scientific "experts" to defend evolution as fact not theory; and denied defense requests to remove the "Read your Bible" banner from the courtroom; or abandon opening prayers in court. Darrow gained a bit of ground by putting Bryan on the stand as a Bible "expert," embarrassing him with questions linking science and creation stories. Raulston declared the case closed and when the jury quickly found Scopes guilty, fined him $100.

---

THE DEACON

When I left for college my youth minister showed all the graduates a movie about this and warned us of just how much of God has been removed from schools since then.

---

On appeal, the Tennessee Supreme Court upheld the anti-evolution law but dismissed the verdict and court fine on a technicality. Case closed? Of course not! Evolution continues to divide certain groups within the church, even as new generations of Christians debate global warming, homosexual and transgender biology, and assorted other Culture Wars. The "circus in Dayton" simply anticipated ideological and educational divisions that are with us yet.[13]

## Roman Catholics and Modernity: A Long March to Religious Liberty

The Roman Catholic Church confronted modernity almost as soon as it appeared on the scene, challenging, often through papal encyclical, the very idea of "progress" as detrimental to order and authority in the church and the world. The Church rejected movements promoting democracy, idealism, individualism, and the idea that religious faith could be distinct from communal or cultural tradition, as in the separation of church and state. The French Revolution, the rise of Napoleon, and efforts of certain European governments to expand control over national churches, also created significant concern in Rome.

In 1862, Pope Pius IX wrote the infamous *Syllabus of Errors*, condemning modernity in its varied expressions including freedoms of press, education, and religion as well as efforts of the secular state to intervene in ecclesiastical affairs, or undermine Church teachings on marriage and divorce. The encyclical concluded with the assertion that the "Roman Pontiff" would never "reconcile himself, and come to terms with progress, liberalism and modern civilization."[14]

---

As a less holy Father, I am glad that no one has chronicled all the embarrassing times I have made declarations of "errors."

**THE ELDER**

---

A century later, Pope John XXIII offered another perspective, acknowledging in *Pacem in Terris* (1963) that "in the modern world human society has taken on an entirely new appearance in the field of social and political life." Pope John also noted the general acceptance of the idea that all persons "are equal by reason of their natural dignity."[15] Thus each person has the natural right to exercise religious faith according to the dictates of conscience—a recognition of religious liberty for all persons, involving the right to engage in religious life both "privately and publicly" as they saw fit.[16] The encyclical sought to move the church toward greater response to, and appreciation for, human rights in multiple areas of modern thought and practice. Its statements on human rights, individual conscience, and religious liberty reflected significant changes from previous pronouncements.

Pope John's views were echoed in the various "Constitutions" of Vatican Council II (1961–1965), including a statement of "General Principles on Religious Liberty," that every individual "has a right to religious freedom." It asserts that no one should be coerced into faith by "any human power" to live and act "contrary to personal beliefs."[17] American priest and theologian John Courtney Murray acknowledged that Catholics came "late" to the principle of religious liberty, and that the statement set forth at Vatican II represented a major change in the Church's response to modernity.[18]

## Democratic Idealism and the Demand for Civil Rights

Modernity increased concerns for civil rights, related to issues of race, economics, sexuality, and women's rights. Efforts to dismantle Jim Crow segregation in the American South, and apartheid in South Africa, divided Christian individuals and communions from the beginning. In those settings, the church was an important and inescapable participant.

## *"Been in the Storm So Long": The Fight against Jim Crow*

In the United States, the end of the Civil War led to Reconstruction, the rise of the Ku Klux Klan, the development of Lost Cause mythology for explaining Southern cultural identity, and the legalization of "separate but equal" societies, black and white, through Jim Crow legislation and social policy. African American churches, long sanctuaries for blacks, North and South, became gathering places for those who challenged an American democracy that had ignored or negated their presence since slavery time.

I grieve just how much ignorance remains present and unacknowledged.

THE BISHOP

Martin Luther King Jr., pastor of the Dexter Avenue Baptist Church in Montgomery, Alabama, and Fannie Lou Hamer, Christian and civil rights leader in Mississippi, illustrate the link between church and democratic idealism in the struggle for liberation. The African American pulpit had long been a sounding board for justice and an end to Jim Crow society. King's leadership of the civil rights movement began not long after his arrival in Montgomery when, on December 1, 1955, Rosa Parks refused to take her seat in the "colored section" of the Cleveland Avenue bus. In the bus boycott that followed, churches became gathering places for African Americans refusing to utilize city transportation, a strategy that ultimately sparked other protests against racial segregation in public facilities and voting rights.

It was dangerous business in which many civil rights protesters, both black and white, were murdered. In *Stride Toward Freedom: The Montgomery Story*, King tells of a religious experience that overcame him at the kitchen table of his home following a threatening phone call warning him to get out of town or face violence on himself and his family. Exhausted and ready to give up, he sat at the table and cast himself on the presence of God. Confessing that "I've come to the point where I can't face it alone," King says that he then experienced an "inner voice" admonishing him to "stand up for righteousness . . . and God will be at your side forever." After that, King wrote, "I was ready to face anything."[19] And he did, enduring dogs, fire hoses, and jail in Birmingham; living long enough to see civil rights legislation become law; and shot down in Memphis in April 1968 while protesting wages and working conditions on behalf of city sanitation employees.

Fannie Lou Hamer, sharecropper and Methodist laywoman, sensed a call to "step out on God's word of promise" in trying to change voting laws in Mississippi in 1962. Her decision took her to the Sunflower County courthouse with a busload of some eighteen African Americans seeking voter registration. Hamer and others were forced to take the infamous "literacy test" of twenty-five questions, including an explanation of obscure passages from Mississippi's state constitution. Of course she failed. On the bus ride home, the driver was arrested for driving a vehicle that looked like a school bus—fake charges, to be sure. The bus riders feared that they too would soon be jailed. Then came the voice of Fannie Lou Hamer, singing out from the back of the bus:

> "Have a little talk with Jesus, Tell him all about our troubles,
> Hear our feeble cry, Answer by and by,
> Feel little prayer wheel turning, Feel a fire a burning
> Just a little talk with Jesus makes it right."[20]

For the sake of voting rights and gospel, Fannie Lou Hamer was ridiculed, harassed, and beaten across the Mississippi Delta, and in many of those terrible moments, she sang, "Just a little talk with Jesus makes it right." For Hamer, faith, justice, and dissent were inseparable.

---

Stories of faith like these are the greatest inspiration and challenge I know. We need to tell and keep telling these saintly narratives.

THE ACOLYTE

---

## An End to Apartheid: South African Churches

In South Africa, apartheid (separateness) began in earnest in 1948 with legislation, not only to require separate public facilities for blacks and whites, but also to segregate blacks into isolated living zones, away from white enclaves. Church leaders such as Anglican Bishop Desmond Tutu joined in the battle against segregationist laws and townships. As a student and later a teacher in black-only schools in South Africa, Tutu saw firsthand the effects of those underfunded educational programs. He also witnessed and opposed the extension of apartheid into every facet of South African life.

After theological studies in South Africa and England, he was ordained a priest, and was invited to teach in several church-related schools. In 1975 he became the first black named as dean of the Johannesburg cathedral, and shortly thereafter was consecrated Bishop of Lesotho. Ultimately, he became Archbishop of Cape Town, the highest Anglican clergy position in the country.[21] In 1985 Tutu received the Nobel Peace Prize for his actions against apartheid and for his nonviolent approach. From those positions Tutu worked tirelessly with other leaders such as Nelson Mandela, who became the first black president of South Africa in 1995, following release from decades of imprisonment and the end of apartheid. He also chaired the Truth and Reconciliation Commission, a group charged with responding to the injustice of apartheid and shaping the future of post-apartheid South African society. In its final report, the Truth and Reconciliation Commission noted that numerous Christian communions "gave their blessing" to the apartheid system. Some even linked apartheid to "the mission of the church." Other faith communities suffered greatly, with persecution visited on their leaders, and their property confiscated. Yet, the report concluded, "Churches, mosques, synagogues and temples—often divided amongst themselves—spawned many of apartheid's strongest foes, motivated by values and norms coming from their particular faith traditions."[22]

---

Truth and Reconciliation are a seriously powerful duo and one that the powerful work hard to suppress.

THE ELDER

---

## Liberation Theology: The Churches as Base Communities

In South America, a social movement known as Liberation Theology took shape as a response to extreme poverty and governmental corruption throughout Latin America. Rooted in such organizations as the Latin American Episcopal Conference (CELAM) formed in 1955 and post-Vatican II gatherings at Medellín, Colombia, and Pueblo, Mexico, in the 1960s, Liberation Theology challenged Roman Catholics to listen and respond to the poverty and oppression that surrounded their often opulent churches and clerical lifestyles. Catholic priest Gustavo Gutiérrez's important work, *A Theology of Liberation: History, Politics, and Salvation*, set forth the basic concerns of the movement. These included:

- "Prophetic denunciation" of injustices present throughout Latin American society.

- A renewal of "conscienticizing evangelization" in the name of a liberating God.
- A mandate for the church to identify with the poor of the world.
- The centrality of Jesus Christ and his concern for the poor.
- A new commitment from Catholic clergy to live with, among, and for the poor, beyond materialism.[23]

---

**THE DEACON**

I love Gutiérrez. He was the first person to break through my anti-world and escapist vision of the faith.

---

Liberation Theology was controversial from the moment it began, challenging the authority of Catholic ecclesiastical hierarchies and governmental leaders, particularly those that oppressed the poor militarily, economically, and spiritually. Church leaders from popes on down were critical of liberationist links to certain Marxist/Socialist viewpoints, challenges to church authority, and efforts to encourage lay leadership in what liberationist Father Leonardo Boff called *comunidades eclesiales de base*. These grassroots, church-based communities, often lay-led, included gatherings for worship, prayer, Bible study, and response to spiritual and political issues, and were viewed by many ecclesiastical and governmental officials as undermining church and state traditions and systems.[24]

The assassination of the Oscar Romero, the Archbishop of San Salvador, in 1980 (while he said Mass) was one of many violent acts related to liberationist religious and political confrontations. Although he distanced himself from Liberation Theology as a movement, Romero was outspoken in his liberationist calls for government reform and justice for all persons, particularly those living in poverty.

---

THE ELDER

When I learned that Romero was murdered by an American-trained and -funded death squad, I knew my identity as a Christian and a citizen was going to be tense.

---

Gustavo Gutiérrez sums up the impact of modernity on church and society when he writes: "Since the Enlightenment, the political order is an order of freedom. The political structures are no longer given, previous to man's freedom, but are rather realities based on freedom, taken on and modified by man. Political freedom is, from that time forward, the history of freedom."[25]

## Liberation and Sex: Not to Be Forgotten

By the 1960s questions of overpopulation and global pollution exacerbated by ever-escalating birthrates, were already being addressed in such books as Rachel Carson's *Silent Spring* (1964) and Paul Ehrlich's *The Population*

*Bomb* (1969). That era also witnessed the appearance of the birth control pill and with it accompanying questions about reproduction, sex, and sexuality. Liberationist ideals extended to the women's rights movement, raising issues related to feminism, reproductive rights, and women in the professions, including ordination of female clergy, all of which presented new possibilities and controversies inside and outside the church.

Roman Catholics were particularly concerned for the ramifications of new reproductive freedom, and offered strong opposition to birth control. In his famous encyclical *Humane Vitae*, released in 1964, Pope Paul VI addressed issues of sex and sexuality, contraception and abortion, marriage and family as no pope had done before, restating earlier pronouncements, while extending traditional teachings in response to the scientific and societal challenges to traditional doctrine and familial practice. The encyclical begins with the pope's acknowledgment that "the most remarkable development" related to modernity and new science "is to be seen in man's stupendous progress in the domination and rational organization of the forces of nature to the point that he is endeavoring to extend this control over every aspect of his own life . . . even over the laws that regulate the transmission of life."[26] The encyclical affirmed that sexual intercourse should be practiced only in marriage, and urged couples to follow "the precepts of the natural law," by which "every marital act must of necessity retain its intrinsic relationship to the procreation of human life."[27] Meaning no use of artificial birth control.

Likewise, global Protestantism experienced parallel divisions, with conservatives reflecting similar concerns

While this position still makes no sense to me, I will say having a close lifelong Catholic friend has helped me understand it.

THE BISHOP

of Roman Catholic and Orthodox Christians; while many liberal Christians pressed for changes or at least expanded options for responding to sexual practices, same-sex relationships and marriage, AIDS/HIV, childrearing, and church policies—all of which created implicit if not explicit schism in most Protestant denominations worldwide.

These and other liberationist issues likewise galvanized ecclesiastical communities, many long divided over the roles of women in the church and the family, issues not only related to husband/wife relationships, but to homosexual relationships as well. By the late twentieth and early twenty-first century, Lesbian-Gay-Bisexual-Transgender (LGBT) individuals came "out of the closet" in increasing numbers, making their sexual orientation public to their families, in the workplace, and in the church. Indeed, ecclesial communions split between those that sought to be "open and affirming" to LGBT persons, and those that insisted that homosexuality was a sexual sin on the order of adultery or fornication. Legal recognition of same-sex marriages in certain western cultures and the ordination of LGBT clergy further divided Christians, in churches and in families.

THE ACOLYTE

The number of eye-rolls my friends have when Christians act a fool about sexuality is very very high. If life-expectancy hadn't grown so much, this issue would be settled. Sorry Grandpa.

In December 2016, Wilshire Baptist Church, Dallas, Texas voted 577 to 367 to extend full membership to LGBT persons, including marriage, baptism, communion, and ordination. The Baptist General Convention of Texas, of which the church was a member, promptly moved to dismiss the congregation from its ranks. A spokesperson for the Baptist Convention noted that, "All Texas Baptists are loving, respectful and welcoming to all people. But while we are welcoming, we are not affirming" of homosexual practice. George Mason, longtime pastor of the Wilshire Church, acknowledged that he reached a point where he could no longer refuse full membership to those whom he had dedicated as children, baptized, and helped nurture into Christian living. He asked, "Am I supposed to tell them that they should be struggling with it? Or am I supposed to tell them that they are loved by God, and ask them to live out their faiths as their full selves? I've come to the conclusion it should be the latter."[28] The divisions related to that one

Texas congregation illustrate the continuing debates and difficulties churches confront, not only regarding sexuality, but the nature of the church itself.

---

George Mason is my new favorite Baptist! Well maybe after Jimmy Carter.

THE DEACON

---

## Future Church: Is Anybody Listening?

The church of Jesus Christ is both united and divided, in Christ; but unable to agree on what exactly that means. It began, perhaps, with the painful decision over whether Gentiles could actually be welcomed into Christ's body, the church. "We, many as we are, are one bread and one body," Paul wrote to the Corinthian church, a community factionalized over preachers, sex, eating habits, and glossolalia (speaking in tongues). Simply add firearms, pollution, and wine at Holy Communion (and dinner), and you've got the church in the modern world! It is a church where the boundaries are at once being extended and receding.

As the twenty-first century takes shape, the Christian world seems divided into what Philip Jenkins labels northern- and southern-hemisphere Christianity. He concludes that "the center of gravity in the Christian world has shifted inexorably southward," in countries that include large numbers of Christians in Africa, Latin America, and Asia, particularly China and South Korea. He writes that

Britain, France, Italy, and Spain would have occupied the top of any 1950 list of leading Christian countries, and predicts that in 2050 none of those nations will be on such a list.[29] A few comparisons illustrate the point. In the United Kingdom, 2015, surveys indicate that some 4.7 percent of the population in England attend church each Sunday; 4.8 percent in Wales; and 8.9 percent in Scotland.[30] That same year, the growth of the church in parts of Asia, Africa, and South America far outpaced traditional Christian groups in the West.

Many western countries posted significant increases in "nones," individuals who claim no religious affiliation or inclination. In the United States, for example, studies done between 2010 and 2016 indicated that those who identified as "nones," long numbering around 7 percent of the population, increased with almost every poll, reaching some 25 percent in 2016, a statistic that made "nones" the largest religious designation in the country. Thus one in

---

THE BISHOP

In my liberal Protestant church of 500 I had over 20 percent of the congregation self-identify as "none." This is why I get frustrated with Bill Maher and the New Atheists using it as a label for their team. Attending and Tithing "nones" aren't atheists.

---

five Americans claimed no affiliation with a specific religious tradition. Some have never had religious affiliation, while others grew up in various religious traditions but have chosen to leave them behind. As the church, north and south, east and west, confronts its future, perhaps it is time to revisit the idea of Re-formation.

## *Ecclesia Semper Reformanda:* The Church Is Always Reforming

"Arise, O Lord (*Exsurge Domine*) and judge thy cause. A wild boar is loose in thy vineyard." That's how Pope Leo X introduced his denunciation of Martin Luther in a papal encyclical released June 15, 1520. The document condemned a variety of Luther's views, including his insistence that "the Roman Pontiff, the successor of Peter, is not the vicar of Christ over all the churches of the entire world"; and that "the burning of heretics is against the will of the Spirit."[31]

It went downhill from there. The encyclical concluded with Leo's demand that the German monk and his followers "recant perpetually such errors and views," and gave them sixty days to cease preaching or publishing their heretical opinions. Should they refuse, the pope would be compelled to "condemn this Martin, his supporters, adherents and accomplices as barren vines which are not in Christ," excommunicating them from Church and salvation. Luther and his students from the University of Wittenberg (founded in 1502) burned the document in the streets.[32] There was no going back. Reformations are often a long time coming (Luther's was), but once they catch fire, watch out.

Some 500 years after Luther posted 95 Theses on the Castle Church door, the Protestant Reformation seems long ago and far away. In 2016, Pope Francis prayed with Swedish Lutherans, urging greater Christian unity and confessing: "We, too, must look with love and honesty at our past, recognizing error and seeking forgiveness." Ecumenical and interfaith dialogue, religious liberty, and declining numbers (at least in the West) create opportunity, even necessity, for greater ecclesiastical cooperation.[33]

---

THE DEACON

I think we are finally getting around to ecumenical unity at the point our youngest members don't care that much about the identity they receive from their denomination.

---

So how might the legacy of early Protestantism inform and re-form the church of today and tomorrow? Here's one short list for continued reflection.

*Re-formation forces us to confront our gospel blind sides.* For Luther, the church's sale of indulgences as a way of easing fear of eternal punishment had become a money-making gimmick that corrupted the nature of the gospel itself. He wrote: "Indulgences are positively harmful to the recipient because they impede salvation by diverting charity and inducing a false sense of security." Rather, Luther said, "he who gives to the poor is better than he who receives an indulgence."[34] Re-formation asks: What actions and ideas do contemporary churches promote and protect that are polluting the gospel here and now?

*Re-formation requires continued quest for and engagement with the word of God, written, preached, and enacted.* In *Luther: An Introduction to His Thought*, Gerhard Ebeling pointed to Luther's belief that all "reformation action" would occur "through the word alone." Luther challenged the church to turn loose the gospel and stop trying to bind Spirit to ecclesiastical structure.[35] He wrote: "All I have done is to put forth, preach and write the word of God, and apart from this I have done nothing. While I have been sleeping, or drinking Wittenberg beer with my friend Philip [Melanchthon], . . . it is the word that has done great things. . . . I have let the word act . . . it is all powerful, it takes hearts prisoner, and when they are taken prisoner, the work that is done comes from the word itself."[36] In the struggle for and with God's elusive word, Scripture and Spirit, heart and head, church and culture are inextricably related. Declaring that word, spoken, written, and enacted, is, Luther believed, what it means to be evangelical. The sacrament of the word remains a reforming witness in the church and the world.

*Re-formation compels Christians to pursue an experience of* ***sola fide***. Faith alone, closely related to the priesthood of all believers, freed individuals to seek grace apart from priestly intervention. But it also forced church and clergy to clarify the nature of faith, articulating ways in which it is secured and retained.

In a 1968 essay called "The Night Spirit and the Dawn Air," Trappist Thomas Merton wrote: "The religious genius of the Protestant Reformation, as I see it, lies in its struggle with the problem of justification in all its depth." In its "simplest form" justification involves the conversion of "the wicked and the sinful to Christ." Yet in its "*most radical form*," justification by faith included a more "problematic" call for the conversion "of the pious and the good." Catholics and Protestants, Merton insisted, could agree that "conversion to Christ is not merely the conversion from bad habits to good habits, but *nova creatura*," transformation into a new creation "in Christ and in the Spirit."[37] Amid twenty-first-century re-formation, Protestants would do well to listen to yet another Catholic monk.

So on their way to the future, Christians (and their churches) might consider this:

When grace becomes an entitlement, not a gift, it's time for Reformation.

When Christians confuse religious liberty with culture-privilege, it's time for Reformation.

When conversion turns into a Jesus vaccination, it's time for Reformation.

When governments claim to speak for Divinity, it's time for Reformation.

When the language of piety obscures justice, compassion, and reconciliation, it's time for Reformation.

When the "wild boars" of a transforming gospel are merely bored or boring, it's time for Reformation.

Let's turn loose the Word.

# Notes

## Chapter One

1. Hippolytus, *Refutation omnium haeresium* viii. 19, in Henry Bettenson, ed., *Documents of the Christian Church* (London: Oxford University Press, 1963), 109.

2. Eusebius, *Ecclesiastical History* V. xvi. 7, in Henry Bettenson, ed., *Documents of the Christian Church*, 109.

3. Frederick Buechner, *The Alphabet of Grace* (New York: Seabury, 1977), 15.

4. https://www.ahdictionary.com/word/search.html?q=irony.

5. Tacitus, *Annales*, xv. 44 in Henry Bettenson, ed., *Documents of the Christian Church*, 2.

6. Christopher Hitchens, *god is not Great: How Religion Poisons Everything* (New York: Twelve, 2007), 118–20.

7. Clifford Geertz, *The Interpretation of Cultures* (New York: Basic Books, 1973), 89.

8. Mark Shorer, "The Necessity of Myth," in *Myth and Mythmakers*, ed. Henry A. Murray (Boston: Beacon, 1960), 355.

9. Rollo May, "Symbolism in Religion and Literature," University of Florida Libraries, https://archive.org/stream/symbolisminrelig00mayr/symbolisminrelig00mayr_djvu.txt, 34, 17.

10. *Didache*, in Edgar J. Goodspeed, *The Apostolic Fathers* (New York: Harper Brothers, 1950), 15–16.

## Chapter Two

1. "The Teaching of the Twelve Apostles," in Edgar J. Goodspeed, *The Apostolic Fathers: An American Translation* (New York: Harper Brothers, 1950), 16.

2. "The First Letter of Clement," in Goodspeed, *The Apostolic Fathers*, 70.

3. Ibid., 71.

4. Ignatius of Antioch, "Letter to the Trallians," in Goodspeed, *The Apostolic Fathers*, 218.

5. Ignatius, "Letter to the Smyrnaeans," in Goodspeed, *The Apostolic Fathers*, 230.

6. W. H. C. Frend, *The Rise of Christianity* (Philadelphia: Fortress Press, 1984), 753–54.

7. Ibid., 760.

8. Ibid.

9. Eusebius, *Ecclesiastical History* Books 1–5 (New York: Fathers of the Church, 1953), 132.

10. *Against the Roman Papacy, an Institution of the Devil*, p. 349 of Luther's Works, vol. 41.

11. Roland Bainton, *Here I Stand* (New York: Mentor, 1950), 181–82.

12. Of the role of the teacher, Calvin wrote: "teachers are not put in charge of discipline, or administering the sacraments, or warnings and exhortations, but only of Scriptural interpretation—to keep doctrine whole and pure among believers." Ibid., 106.

13. John Calvin, *The Institutes of the Christian Religion*, IV. iii.4.

14. "Declaration of Faith of English People, 1611," in William L. Lumpkin, *Baptist Confessions of Faith*, 2nd rev. edition (Valley Forge, PA: Judson, 2011), 112.

15. William R. Estep Jr., *The Anabaptist Story* (Nashville: Broadman, 1963), 11.

16. Tertullian, *De Praescriptione Haereticorum*, xx, xxi, in Henry Bettenson, *Documents of the Christian Church* (London: Oxford University Press, 1963), 99.

17. Tertullian, *De Exhortatione Castitatis*, 7, in Bettenson, *Documents of the Christian Church*, 100.

18. Robert Barclay, *The Chief Principles of the Christian religion, as professed by the people called Quakers*, in Bettenson, *Documents of the Christian Church*, 355, 359.

19. Bill J. Leonard, "Good News from Wolf Creek," *Christian Century*, May 2, 1984, 455.

## Chapter Three

1. Bart D. Ehrman, *Lost Christianities* (Oxford: Oxford University Press, 2003), 163–64.

2. Ibid., 164.

3. Joseph H. Lynch, *Early Christianity: A Brief History* (Oxford: Oxford University Press, 2010), 54–58.

4. Irenaeus, *Against Heresies I.I.II*, in J. Stevenson, ed., *A New Eusebius* (London: SPCK, 1970), 89–90.

5. Clement of Alexandria, *Stromateis*, III.7.59.3, in Stevenson, ed., *A New Eusebius*, 91.

6. Justin Martyr, *The First Apology*, in Thomas B. Falls, ed., *The Fathers of the Church* (New York: Christian Heritage, 1948), 83–84.

7. Ibid., 84.

8. Bradley P. Nystrom and David P. Nystrom, *The History of Christianity: An Introduction* (Boston: McGraw-Hill, 2004), 89.

9. Ibid.

10. Hippolytus, *Against Noetus*, I, in J. Stevenson, ed., *A New Eusebius*, 159.

11. Ibid.

12. Ibid.

13. Cyprian, *On the Unity of the Catholic Church*, https://www.christianhistoryinstitute.org/study/module/cyprian/.

14. See http://mluther.ccws.org/stand/1.html.

15. *Exsurge Domine*, "Papal Encyclicals Online, http://www.papalencyclicals.net/Leo10/l10exdom.htm.

16. Leo X, *Decet Romanum*, http://bookofconcord.org/decet-romanum.php.

17. "St. Thomas More," *Catholic Encyclopedia*, http://www.newadvent.org/cathen/14689c.htm.

18. Bertolt Brecht, *Galileo* (New York: Grove, 1966), 49.

19. Dava Sobel, *Galileo's Daughter: A Historical Memoir of Science, Faith, and Love* (New York: Walker, 1999).

20. Ibid., 78.

21. Brecht, *Galileo*, 73.

22. Ibid., 89.

23. Sobel, *Galileo's Daughter*, 276.

24. Brecht, *Galileo*, 129.

25. See also Bill J. Leonard, "Gawking Is Not Seeing," Baptist News Global, November 4, 2015, https://baptistnews.com/article/gawking-is-not-seeing/. Used by permission.

## Chapter Four

1. Arthur Huff Fauset, *Sojourner Truth: God's Faithful Pilgrim* (Chapel Hill: University of North Carolina Press, 1938), 137.

2. http://www.newadvent.org/cathen/07674d.htm.

3. "The Church," in *Documents of Vatican II*, ed. Walter M. Abbott (New York: New Win, 1966), 92–93.

4. Augustine, *Literal Commentary on Genesis*, in Elizabeth Clark, *Women in the Early Church* (Collegeville, MN: Liturgical, 1983), 40.

5. Rosemary Radford Ruether, *Religion and Sexism* (New York: Simon & Schuster, 1974), 156.

6. Ibid.

7. Ibid.

8. Ibid., 157.

9. Tertullian, *On the Dress of Women*, in Elizabeth Clark, *Women in the Early Church*, 39.

10. Ruether, *Religion and Sexism*, 158.

11. Ibid., 160.

12. Augustine, *On Marriage and Concupiscence*, in Elizabeth Clark, *Women in the Early Church*, 55.

13. Ruether, *Religion and Sexism*, 166–68.

14. Augustine, *On Marriage and Concupiscence*, 60.

15. Ruether, *Religion and Sexism*, 166–68.

16. Augustine, *On Marriage and Concupiscence*, in *Women in the Early Church*, 60.

17.Jerome, *Against Jovian*, in Elizabeth Clark, *Women in the Early Church*, 129.

18. Ibid., 126.

19. Jerome, *Letter 22* (to Eustochium), in Elizabeth Clark, *Women in the Early Church*, 131; and Ruether, *Religion and Sexism*, 174.

20. Jerome, *Letter 107* (to Laeta), http://www.tertullian.org/fathers2/NPNF2-06/Npnf2-06-03.htm#P3757_1005453.

21. Ruether, *Religion and Sexism*, 17.

22. Ibid., 222.

23. Ibid., 223.

24. Ibid., 229.

25. Elizabeth A. Johnson, *She Who Is: The Mystery of God in Feminist Theological Discourse* (New York: Crossroad, 1998), 25.

26. Ibid., 24.

27. Umphrey Lee, *The Lord's Horseman: John Wesley the Man* (Nashville: Abingdon, 1954), 19.

28. "From Mrs. Susanna Wesley," August 19, 1724, in *The Works of John Wesley, Volume 25, Letters I 1721-1739* (Oxford: Clarendon, 1980), 148.

29. "A Brief Confession or Declaration of Faith" (1660), in *Baptist Confessions of Faith*, 2nd rev. edition, ed. William L. Lumpkin and Bill J. Leonard (Valley Forge, PA: Judson, 2011), 209–10.

30. *Testimonies of the Life, Character, Revelations and Doctrines of Mother Ann Lee and the Elders with Her, with Whom the Word of Eternal Life Was Opened* (Albany, NY: Weed, Parsons & Co, 1888), 5–6.

31. Julian of Norwich, *Revelations of Divine Love* (New York: Penguin, 1998), 140.

32. Abby Stoner, "Sisters Between: Gender and the Medieval Beguines," http://www2.kenyon.edu/projects/margin/beguine1.htm.

33. Sor Juana de la Cruz, *Poems, Protest, and a Dream* (New York: Penguin, 1997), xxxv.

34. Ilan Stavans, Introduction, in *Poems, Protest, and a Dream*, xli.

35. Michelle A. Gonzalez, *Sor Juana: Beauty and Justice in the Americas* (Maryknoll, NY: Orbis, 2003), 116.

36. Sor Juana de la Cruz, *Loa for the Auto sacramental*, in *Poems, Protest, and a Dream*, 217.

37. Jarena Lee, *The Life and Religious Experience of Jarena Lee, a Coloured Lady, Giving an Account of her call to Preach the Gospel*, in *Sisters of the Spirit: Three Black Women's Autobiographies of the Nineteenth Century*, ed. William L. Andrews (Bloomington: Indiana University Press, 1986), 29.

38. Ibid., 33–34.

39. Ibid., 35.

40. Ibid., 36.

41. Ibid., 5–6.

42. Ibid., 37.

43. For more information, see Christine Trevett, *Montanism: Gender, Authority and the New Prophecy* (Cambridge: Cambridge University Press, 1996).

44. Donald G. Mathews, *Religion in the Old South* (Chicago: University of Chicago Press, 1977), 110.

45. Ibid., 113.

46. Ibid., 112–13.

47. Johnson, *She Who Is*, 31–32.

## Chapter Five

1. William Cowper, "There Is a Fountain," in *The Baptist Hymnal* (Nashville: Convention Press, 1991), 142.

2. Justin, *Apology I*, in J. Stevenson, ed., *A New Eusebius* (London: SPCK, 1970), 65.

3. Tertullian, *De praescriptione haereticorum*, in Henry Bettenson, *Documents of the Christian Church* (Oxford: Oxford University Press, 1969), 8.

4. *Didache*, VII, 1–4, in *A New Eusebius*, 126.

5. Cyril of Jerusalem, *On the Mysteries II*, http://www.newadvent.org/fathers/310120.htm.

6. Martin Luther, "Part Fourth, On Infant Baptism," *The Larger Catechism*, http://www.iclnet.org/pub/resources/text/wittenberg/luther/catechism/web/cat-13a.html.

7. John Calvin, *Institutes of the Christian Religion*, http://www.theologian.org.uk/doctrine/calvin-baptism.html.

8. Justin, *Apology I*, in *A New Eusebius*, 67.

9. Thomas Aquinas, *Summa Theologica*, iii. Q. lxxv, Article IV, in Bettenson, *Documents of the Christian Church*, 208.

10. *The canons and decrees of the sacred and oecumenical Council of Trent*, trans. J. Waterworth (London: Dolman, 1848), 53, see http://history.hanover.edu/texts/trent/ct07.html.

11. Ulrich Zwingli (*Works* IV, 14, 12–15), cited in Peter Opitz, "At the Table of the Lord: To Zwingli's View of the Lord's Supper," https://www.academia.edu/5802889/At_the_Table_of_the_Lord_To_Zwinglis_View_on_the_Lords_Supper.

12. Opitz, "At the Table of the Lord."

13. John Calvin, *Institutes of the Christian Religion*, vol. II (Edinburgh: T&T Clark, 1863), 564.

14. William James, *The Varieties of Religious Experience* (New York: Modern Library, 1902), 79–80.

15. Ibid., 186.

16. "A Declaration of Faith," in *Baptist Confessions of Faith*, 2nd rev. edition, ed. William Lumpkin and Bill J. Leonard (Valley Forge, PA: Judson, 2012), 111.

17. Bill J. Leonard, *A Sense of the Heart: Christian Religious Experience in the United States* (Nashville: Abingdon, 2014).

18. The Yoido Full Gospel Church in Korea claims over 800,000 members, and is associated with the Assemblies of God. Pentecostals are the fastest-growing religious group in South America; the Reynolda Church (Presbyterian) in Winston-Salem, NC is known by many as a "charismatic Presbyterian" congregation.

19. Philip Jenkins, *The Next Christendom: The Coming of Global Christianity* (New York: Oxford University Press, 2002), 215.

## Chapter Six

1. William R. Estep, *The Anabaptist Story* (Nashville: Broadman, 1963), 62–63.

2. Bill J. Leonard, "Louisville and Orlando 2016," *Baptist News Global*, June 16, 2016. The material on Ali was previously published in this essay.

3. http://www.merriam-webster.com/dictionary/dissent.

4. Edwin Scott Gaustad, *Dissent in American Religion* (Chicago: University of Chicago Press, 1973), 2.

5. Ibid., 4.

6. Ibid., 5.

7. Ibid., 7.

8. Ibid.

9. Elizabeth Clark, *Women in the Early Church* (Collegeville, MN: Liturgical, 1983), 97.

10. Ibid., 100.

11. *Oxford English Dictionary* (online edition, 1989).

12. Firmicus Maternus, *On the Error of Profane Religions*, in Roger Pearse, "The spirit of persecution in Firmicus Maternus," http://www.roger-pearse.com/weblog/2009/11/10/the-spirit-of-persecution-in-firmicus-maternus/.

13. Joseph H. Lynch, *Early Christianity: A Brief History* (Oxford: Oxford University Press, 2010), 137–38.

14. Balthasar Hubmaier, *Concerning Heretics and those who Burn them*, in William R. Estep Jr., *Anabaptist Beginnings (1523-1533)* (Nieuwkoop: B. De Graaf, 1976), 53, 51.

15. "A Declaration of Faith of English People," in William L. Lumpkin and Bill J. Leonard, eds., *Baptist Confessions of Faith*, rev. ed. (Valley Forge, PA: Judson, 2011), 111.

16. *Toleration Act, 1689*, http://www.jacobite.ca/documents/1689toleration.htm.

17. Edwin S. Gaustad, *Liberty of Conscience: Roger Williams in America* (Grand Rapids: Eerdmans, 1991), 29.

18. Ibid., 96.

19. Roger Williams, "Mr. Cotton's Letter Lately Printed" (1644) Complete Works (Narragansett), vol. I, 319.

20. William Warren Sweet, *The Story of Religion in America* (Chicago: University of Chicago Press), 69.

21. Bill J. Leonard, *Baptist Ways: A History* (Valley Forge, PA: Judson, 2003), 76–77. See also Bill J. Leonard, *Word of God Across the Ages: Using Church History in Preaching*, third expanded edition (Macon, GA: Smyth & Helwys, Publishing, Inc., 2015), 103–11.

22. Ibid.

23. Bill J. Leonard, "Louisville and Orlando 2016," *Baptist News Global*, June 16, 2016.

## Chapter Seven

1. Joan Chittister, *The Rule of Benedict: Insights for the Ages* (New York: Crossroad, 1997), 19–20.

2. Roger Gottlieb, *Spirituality: What It Is and Why It Matters* (Oxford: Oxford University Press, 2013), 13–14.

3. Chittister, *Rule of Benedict*, 20.

4. Karen E. Smith, *Christian Spirituality* (London: SCM, 2007), 16.

5. J. G. Davies, *The Early Christian Church* (New York: Anchor, 1967), 324–25.

6. Ibid., 246.

7. Chittister, *Rule of Benedict*, 89.

8. Ibid., 19.

9. "Monastic Vows," St. John's Abbey, http://www.abbeyvocations.com/virtual-vocation-office/faq/monastic-vows-qanda/.

10. William James, *The Varieties of Religious Experience* (New York: Modern Library, 1929), 371.

11. Ibid., 372.

12. Ibid.

13. Teresa of Avila, *The Life of Teresa of Jesus* (Garden City, NY: Image, 1960), 274.

14. Ibid., 274–75.

15. Ibid., 366–68.

16. James, *The Varieties of Religious Experience*, 403–4.

17. Catherine Tumber and Walter Earl Fluker, eds., *A Strange Freedom: The Best of Howard Thurman on Religious Experience and Public Life* (Boston: Beacon, 1998), 3–4.

18. Howard Thurman, *With Head and Heart* (New York: Harvest, 1979), 74.

19. Bill J. Leonard, *A Sense of the Heart: Christian Religious Experience in the U.S.* (Nashville: Abingdon, 2014), 301–4.

20. Rufus Jones, *The Testimony of the Soul* (New York: Macmillan, 1936), 43–44.

21. Ibid., 41–42, 44.

22. Howard Thurman, "Prayer," in Tumber and Fluker, *A Strange Freedom*, 81.

23. Ibid.

24. Ibid., 89.

25. Ibid., 243.

26. Ibid., 244–45.

27. Ibid., 27–29.

28. Jones, *The Testimony of the Soul*, 202.

29. Ibid., 208.

30. Thich Nhat Hanh, *Living Buddha, Living Christ* (New York: Riverhead, 1995), 14.

31. Richard R. Niebuhr, cited in Phil Cousineau, *The Art of Pilgrimage: The Seeker's Guide to Making Travel Sacred* (Boston: Conari, 1998), 14.

## Chapter Eight

1. Amanda Porterfield, *Modern Christianity to 1900* (Minneapolis: Fortress Press, 2007), 1.

2. Ibid., 3.

3. "Postmodernism," Mary Klages, willamette.edu/~rloftus/postmod.htm.

4. Shailer Mathews, *The Faith of Modernism* (New York: Macmillan, 1924), 21.

5. Ibid., 4.

6. "The Christocentric Liberal Tradition," in H. Shelton Smith, Robert T. Handy, Lefferts A. Loetscher, *American Christianity: An Historical Interpretation with Representative Documents* (New York: Charles Scribner's Sons, 1963), 256.

7. J. Gresham Machen, *Christianity and Liberalism* (Grand Rapids: Eerdmans, 1923), 6–7.

8. Philip J. Lee, *Against the Protestant Gnostics* (New York: Oxford University Press, 1987), 180.

9. George M. Marsden, *Fundamentalism and American Culture* (New York: Oxford University Press, 1980), 3–32.

10. George M. Marsden, *Understanding Fundamentalism and Evangelicalism* (Grand Rapids: Eerdmans, 1991), 1.

11. Jeffrey P. Moran, *The Scopes Trial: A Brief History with Documents* (Boston: Bedford/St. Martin's), 122.

12. Moran, *The Scopes Trial*, 89.

13. Edward J. Larson, *Summer for the Gods: The Scopes Trial and America's Continuing Debate over Science and Religion* (New York: Basic Books, 1997). For fun read H. L. Mencken, *A Religious Orgy in Tennessee* (Hoboken, NJ: Melville House, 1925). Mencken was one of the most famous columnists of his day.

14. "The Syllabus of Errors Condemned by Pius IX," in Papal Encyclicals Online, http://www.papalencyclicals.net/Pius09/p9syll.htm.

15. "*Pacem in Terris Encyclical of John XXIII*," in Papal Encyclicals Online, http://www.papalencyclicals.net/John23/j23pacem.htm.

16. Ibid.

17. “General Principle of Religious Freedom,” in *Documents of Vatican II*, ed. Walter Abbott (New York: Guild Press, 1966), 678.

18. Ibid., 673. See also John Courtney Murray, “On Religious Freedom,” *America* (November 30, 1963), http://www.americamagazine.org/issue/100/religious-liberty.

19. Martin Luther King Jr., *Stride Toward Freedom: The Montgomery Story* (New York: Harper & Row, 1958), 114–15.

20. Charles Marsh, *God’s Long Summer: Stories of Race and Civil Rights* (Princeton: Princeton University Press, 1997), 12–15.

21. “Desmond Tutu,” in *Bio*. http://www.biography.com/people/desmond-tutu-9512516#rise-to-prominence.

22. Truth and Reconciliation Final Report, Volume 4, Chapter 3, 59ff., http://www.justice.gov.za/trc/report/finalreport/Volume%204.pdf.

23. Gustavo Gutiérrez, *A Theology of Liberation: History, Politics, and Salvation* (Maryknoll, NY: Orbis, 1973), 114–18. See also Bill J. Leonard, “*Comunidades Eclesiales de Base* and Autonomous Local Churches: Catholic Liberationists Meet Baptist Landmarkers,” in *Poverty and Ecclesiology: Nineteenth-Century Evangelicals in the Light of Liberation Theology*, ed. Anthony L. Dunnavant (Collegeville, MN: Liturgical, 1992), 71.

24. Leonard, “*Comunidades Eclesiales de Base* and Autonomous Local Churches,” 71–73.

25. Gutiérrez, *A Theology of Liberation*, 221.

26. “Encyclical Letter *Humanae Vitae* of the Supreme Pontiff Paul VI,” http://w2.vatican.va/content/paul-vi/en/encyclicals/documents/hf_p-vi_enc_25071968_humanae-vitae.html.

27. Ibid.

28. Julie Zauzmer, “A church voted to perform gay marriages, and it’s getting kicked out of the Texas Baptists,” *Washington Post*, November 16, 2016, https://www.washingtonpost.com/news/acts-of-faith/wp/2016/11/16/a-dallas-church-voted-to-perform-gay-marriages-and-just-got-kicked-out-of-the-texas-baptists/?utm_term=.558efb86ef25.

29. Philip Jenkins, *The Next Christendom: The Coming of Global Christianity* (New York: Oxford University Press, 2002), 2.

30. UK Christianity 2005–2025, “Faith Survey,” https://faithsurvey.co.uk/uk-christianity.html.

31. Pope Leo X, *Exsurge Domine*, June 15, 1520, http://www.papalencyclicals.net/Leo10/l10exdom.htm.

32. Ibid.

33. Andrew Medichini, Jan M. Olsen, and Nicole Winfield, "Pope Francis prays with Lutherans in Sweden to mark Luther's Protest," October 31, 2016, http://www.washingtontimes.com/news/2016/oct/31/pope-francis-arrives-sweden-mark-luthers-reforms/.

34. Roland Bainton, *Here I Stand: A Life of Martin Luther* (New York: Mentor, 1950), 62–63.

35. Gerhard Ebeling, *Luther: An Introduction to His Thought* (Philadelphia: Fortress Press, 1970), 69.

36. Ibid., 66–67.

37. Thomas Merton, "The Night Spirit and the Dawn Air," in *Conjectures of a Guilty Bystander* (Garden City, NY: Image, 1968), 168–69. See also Bill J. Leonard, "*Exsurge Domine:* Pursuing Re-formation," November 3, 2016, Baptist News Global, https://baptistnews.com/article/exerge-domine-pursuing-re-formation/#.WFBZCvkrLb0.